MW01069034

WE STOOD OUR GROUND: LEXINGTON IN THE FIRST YEAR OF THE AMERICAN REVOLUTION (2ND EDITION)

Alexander R. Cain

2

ISBN #: 978-1-312-43896-5

Content ID: 15107205

Book Title: We Stood Our Ground

© Copyright 2014 by Alexander R. Cain

To my wife Paula

4

Table of Contents

5

PROLOGUE

In the early hours of April 19, 1775, militiamen from Captain John Parker's Company assembled on their village green to await the arrival of the British expedition from Boston to concord. Approximately seventy-seven nervous citizen soldiers stood in ragged lines as countless columns of red-coated Regulars carrying muskets with fixed bayonets quickly marched up Boston Road towards them. When the two forces met, the encounter was brief but bloody. Yet the long term effects of this skirmish were monumental. By the time the King's troops had resumed their march towards Concord, the machinery of the American Revolution had been set in motion.

For over two hundred and thirty years, the Lexington militia has been held to the highest standard by American society. The courage of these men has been extolled countless times in poems, monuments, songs, plays, pageants, film and historical reenactments. Indeed, the events that took place on April 19, 1775 have come to symbolize America's resolve never to submit to political or military tyranny.

Unfortunately, despite the stature the Lexington "Minute Men" have obtained in historical lore, little has been written about their daily lives, the societal structure of their village or even their role in the Siege of Boston. In addition, myth, legend and fantasy clouds much of what we do know about the average Lexington resident. There is even confusion concerning the unit designation by which they are commemorated: Lexington Minute Men.

We Stood Our Ground: Lexington in the First Year of the American Revolution was not written to retell the story of the Battles of Lexington and Concord. Instead, the goals of this book are to shed light onto the world of 18th Century

Lexington and to challenge some of the distortions and assumptions surrounding Lexington. *We Stood Our Ground* is the result of two decades of intensive research in which diaries, depositions, letters, artifacts and other material culture were consulted. Secondary sources were utilized only when necessary.

~ Alexander R. Cain

ACKNOWLEDGEMENTS

I would like to take this opportunity to thank the following individuals and organizations for their assistance and support in publishing the 2nd Edition of *We Stood Our Ground*: Dr. David Hackett Fischer, whose work, *Paul Revere's Ride* still remains highly relevant and guided me as I toiled away at revising my own work. Bill Poole, my father-in-law Vincent Norton and my mother, Patricia Cain, who reviewed, rewrote, criticized and challenged my work on more than one occasion. The Lexington Historical Society for providing me with access to documentation and research not available to the public. Sam Doran for sharing his extensive knowledge and expertise on Lexington and its military and societal culture. Mike DaRu, William Rose, John Nichols and Bruce Leader for sharing their research findings on 18th Century Lexington and Middlesex County. Greg Hurley, Joel Bohy Greg Theberge, Niels Hobbs and the park rangers at Minute Man National Historical Park for raising and improving research standards and the sharing of 18th Century material culture over the last decade since the 1st Edition was published. The Lexington Minute Men, a historical organization dedicated to honoring the participants of the Battle of Lexington for pushing me to update my book. My son John for always provided much needed laughter and my daughter Abigail for always showing interest in the American Revolution. Finally, special thanks to my wife Paula who not only supported and encouraged me throughout this project, but also put up with my many irrelevant stories about the Battle of Lexington and Captain John Parker's Company.

9

~1~

Eighteenth Century Lexington:
A Web of Interdependence

The Village of Lexington was known until 1713 as Cambridge Farms and was located northwest of Boston, nestled among the surrounding towns Menotomy (now Arlington), Bedford, Lincoln, Waltham and Woburn. Sprawled out over nineteen square miles, Lexington consisted of approximately 10,000 acres of fertile fields, gentle hills, woodlands, and peat bogs, crossed by gently meandering streams that eventually found their way to either the Charles or Mystic Rivers.[1] In 1711, at the suggestion of Samuel Stone, great-grandfather of Captain John Parker, the residents of Lexington purchased from Massachusetts Bay Colony an acre and a half of land where the Concord, Bedford and Boston Roads met. From this resolution, a village common

---

[1] Arthur Bernon Tourtellot, *William Diamond's Drum: The Beginning of the War of the American Revolution*, (New York, New York: W.W. Norton and Company, 1959), 30.

was created that instantly became the physical, political, religious and military center of town.[2]

The Common, or "Green" as it was sometimes called, was roughly triangular in shape. It was bounded on the south by the road to Concord running southeast to southwest, on the east by the road to Bedford, and on the north by a narrow dirt track joining the Bedford and Concord Roads. Buckman's Tavern, its stables and adjacent outbuildings stood directly across the Bedford Road from the easternmost point of the common. Built in 1710, the structures functioned to accommodate drovers bringing herds to market in Boston, as well as Lexington residents attending Sunday services or town meetings.

Across the Bedford Road from the tavern, in the angle formed by the Bedford and Concord Roads, stood the town's meetinghouse. The first meetinghouse was erected in 1692, but had been replaced by a larger structure in 1713, the year the town was incorporated. A great barn-like structure with two tiers of galleries and a main floor made up of high walled pews, it served as a town hall, church, an assembly place and an arsenal. Approximately four hundred feet behind the meetinghouse was a schoolhouse, where from October to March, the children of Lexington were instructed in the basic skills of writing and reading by underpaid Harvard graduates or the town minister. To the rear of the meetinghouse, on the south side of the common, stood the belfry. Once used to warn residents of possible attacks by the French and Native Americans, it had functioned for decades for the more peaceful purpose of summoning the residents to church or town meetings.[3]

---

[2] The practice of naming a road according to the direction one is traveling is one that continues to this day in some New England towns. Thus the road to Concord and the Boston Road were one and the same, but the name changed at the Common.

[3] Also on the common were a water well and a stock. Across from the eastern point and behind the meetinghouse were horse sheds. Across from the western point of the common stood an animal pound, used to harbor

The home of Marrett Monroe was located on the south side of the Concord Road across from the Common, while the homes occupied by Daniel and Jonathan Harrington and their families were north of the Common along the narrow dirt lane connecting Bedford Road to Concord Road.[4] In addition to Buckman Tavern and the Monroe and Harrington homes, the only other edifices within the vicinity of the Common were the William Munroe house and some stables, both located on the south side of the road, a little east of the Common in the direction of Boston.

There were two small clusters of homes east of the center of Lexington on the road to Boston. On the north side of the road and along the west bank of Vine Brook, which bisected Boston Road from northeast to southwest, were Amos Muzzy's home and barn. Further east, between Vine Brook and the road to Woburn, were Benjamin Estabrook's house and mill on the north side of the road, and the homes of Jonathan Smith and Benjamin Merriam on the south side. Matthew Mead's home was located in the angle formed by the roads to Boston and Woburn, while Joshua Loring's house was a bit further east on the south side of the Boston Road. The second cluster of homes was further east on the Boston Road, well south of the Woburn Road, and centered near Sergeant William Munroe's Tavern. Residents included Joshua Bond, Nathaniel Mulliken's widow Lydia, Samuel Sanderson, John Mason and John Raymond.

Although several families had lived in Lexington for generations, most of the population was made up of newcomers, seeking to exchange their lives in Boston or Salem for better ones in Lexington. From the 1640's onward, Lexington's population grew by one hundred people per decade.[5] This population "boom" had a direct impact upon the natural and social environment of the town. As new residents

---

escaped livestock.

[4] Next to Daniel Harrington's House was his blacksmith shop.

[5] Tourtellot, 31.

moved in, more woods were cleared, fields cultivated and rich peat swamps harvested.[6] This process continued for over a century until the French Wars of the 1750's, when immigration virtually stopped. By 1775, Lexington was inhabited by over one hundred families that included seven hundred and fifty people, five slaves and four hundred cows.[7]

Many of the townsmen subscribed to "mixed husbandry" farming, which encouraged farmers to produce a variety of items necessary for survival. Such items included vegetables and fruit, meat and wood for fuel and shelter. To generate such supplies for the long term, Lexington farmers needed approximately sixty acres of land. According to research conducted by historian Mary Babson Fuhrer, approximately two to four acres of land was allocated to an orchard and home. The average Lexington family burned about an acre of wood per year. As a result, an additional twenty to thirty acres of land was set aside as a "wood lot".[8] Another six acres were designated as "tillage", which was designed to generate grains for bread and flax for linen. However, to remain productive, tillage needed to be fertilized with cow manure.[9]

Naturally cows needed to be fed. At least fifteen acres of land was usually set aside as grazing fields while another fifteen acres was designated for hay to feed cows and other livestock during the winter months. Of course, cows and other livestock also served as a valuable source of meat, dairy and hides.[10]

On the eve of the American Revolution, farmers in Lexington had roughly allocated ten percent of their lands as

---

[6] *Ibid.*

[7] *Ibid*, 30.

[8] Mary Babson Fuhrer, *The Revolutionary Worlds of Lexington and Concord Compared*, The New England Quarterly, vol. LXXXV, no. 1 (March, 2012), 82.

[9] *Ibid.*

[10] *Ibid.*

tillage, twenty-five percent as pastures and hay fields and forty percent as wood lot. More specifically, according to a 1771 tax valuation of Lexington land, 15.1 acres of land for tillage, 12.5 acres of land for pastures, 14.7 acres of land for hay fields, 21.5 "unimproved acres" or woodlots, and 32.3 acres of "improved acres".[11]

Yet despite the practice of mixed husbandry, the town was not a collection of self-sufficient farms.[12] There was a great interdependence among the residents of Lexington. Cooperation and mutual welfare were common customs in Massachusetts towns and villages. Residents assisted each other with a variety of tasks and in a number of emergencies: preparing meals, building homes, plowing, felling timber, caring for one another when ill or injured or simply offering counsel and advice.[13]

This concept of interdependence spilled over into Lexington's economy as well. When goods or services were exchanged, cash was rarely utilized.[14] Instead, transactions on the local level were recorded in the form of debts and credits. Debts were listed in terms of monetary value and recorded by creditors in account books.[15] At any given time, a yeoman would be both a creditor and a debtor to dozens of his neighbors.[16] Economic success not only required tolerant creditors, but shrewd debtors able to avoid settlement too quickly or frequently.[17] Manual labor was the service most

---

[11] *Ibid.* A review of livestock from the 1771valuation suggests that the average Lexington farmer also had 1.1 horses, 1.4 oxen, 5.1 cows, 3 goats or sheep and 2.2 swine.

[12] Fred Anderson, *A People's Army: Massachusetts Soldiers and Society in the Seven Years War*, (London, England: W.W. Norton and Company, 1984), 28.

[13] Alice Morse Earle, *Home Life in Colonial Days*, (Stockbridge, Massachusetts: House Publishers, 1898), 389-391.

[14] *Ibid.*

[15] *Ibid.*

[16] *Ibid*, 30.

frequently exchanged on the local level.[18] If there was either individual need or general demand for items that could not be produced locally (such as gunpowder, high-grade cloth and pins)[19], Lexington citizens would travel to other towns such as Boston, Salem, Worcester or Newburyport to obtain them.[20]

Because of this economic system, the web of interdependency was strengthened and families continued to rely heavily on one another. The economy thus served as powerful social cement promoting community cooperation and neighborly behavior at all levels.

The extent of cooperation did, however, have limits. The increase in Lexington's population in the mid-18th Century, coupled with a fixed supply of land available as an inheritance forced many young men in Lexington to seek land north or west of Lexington, purchase smaller tracts of land inside Lexington or share with their brothers a divided inheritance.

Many Lexington residents were saddled with

---

[17] *Ibid.* Yet it would be wrong to assume that cash was non-existent in 18th century Massachusetts. As early as 1652, Massachusetts was minting its own coin. Known as the Pine Tree Shilling, the coin was accepted throughout the colonies and as far away as Barbados. Over the next several decades, paper money crept into Massachusetts, replacing the Pine Tree Shilling and creating inflation. Furthermore, the paper money caused the standard to be based not on the English pound, but the Spanish dollar. In 1745, following the capture of Louisbourg from the French, Massachusetts was reimbursed by Parliament in silver for the expedition. As a result, the colony's old paper currency (old tenor) was replaced with a new one (new tenor). By 1773, all Massachusetts paper money had been paid in coin and retired. Beth Gilgun, *Tidings from the 18th Century*, (Texarkana, Texas: Rebel Publishing, 1993), 217-219.

[18] *Ibid*, 29.

[19] *Ibid.*

[20] Fuhrer, 86. Although the Lexington economy was based on agriculture, farmers did have a few opportunities for generating cash through side crafts. In 1774, Lexington boasted, among other trades, two blacksmiths, four wheelwrights and three clock makers. [20] John Parker was a woodworker and fought some success in the production of farm tools

overwhelming debt. In 1759, fifteen percent of Lexington men saw a forced sale of all or part of their real estate to settle at the time of their death. By 1779, the percentage had risen to twenty-nine percent. By the end of the American Revolution, a staggering forty percent of Lexington estates faced forced sales.[21]

Although society in 18th century Lexington was fluid, it was not as mobile as modern society. Residents of Lexington, like most New Englanders, believed that the upper orders of society were to rule, while the lower were expected to obey. Lower class citizens were viewed with contempt and disdain if they attempted to assert influence or power beyond that expected of their station, and were quickly reminded of their proper place in society. Leaders had to be men of distinction, respected by all. By 18th century standards, failure to adhere to this societal structure would not only result in disorder, chaos and anarchy, but would also anger God.[22]

The clergy stood at the pinnacle of 18th century Lexington society. Due to their own considerable talents, and bolstered by the religious doctrine of the 17th century, the Reverend John Hancock[23] and his successor as pastor, Jonas Clarke[24], were the most important individuals in Lexington society. As ministers, they were the spiritual and moral leaders, the political commentators and when the town was without a schoolteacher, the educators as well. The minister held an unchallenged position within society. The citizens of Lexington were expected to entertain him when he called upon them to appear at his home.

---

[21] Fuhrer, 94.

[22] The 1774 Tax Valuations of Lexington suggest the wealthiest resident of Lexington, William Reed, Esq., was assessed 16 shillings, one pence. The town's poorest resident, Ephraim Winship, was assessed a mere ten pence.

[23] The Reverend John Hancock served as pastor of the Church of Christ from 1698 to 1752.

[24] The Reverend Jonas Clarke served as pastor of the Church of Christ from 1753 to 1805.

The minister's function was to help maintain stability and order within Lexington. Thus, he frequently set aside his personal needs for the benefit of Lexington as a whole. Jonas Clarke received a very generous salary, but he often donated part of it to Lexington at the yearly town meetings.[25] In times of need, citizens naturally turned to the minister for assistance. Frequently he involved himself in settling the daily squabbles that arose between residents. Reverend Hancock often settled land disputes by driving a stake into the ground and telling the involved parties that the stake was the borderline and there would be no further quarrel about it.[26] The minister even influenced the education of the town's children, taking a leading role in preparing Lexington boys for Harvard.[27]

Below the ministers stood the selectmen and other town leaders. These were the substantial yeomen and tradesmen who usually had greater wealth and held more property than the average Lexington farmer. These leaders were viewed as role models for the doctrine that ultimately success could only be attained through hard work. Their positions also entitled them to other benefits, including first choice in the purchase of family pews and burial plots, and the right to represent Lexington, first in the House of Representatives in Boston and later in the Massachusetts Provincial Congress.

Individuals rarely exercised local political leadership until they had reached middle life and achieved economic independence.[28] It was assumed that only those who had established a place in society, whose accumulation of property ensured that their interests were dependant on no man, could

---

[25] Tourtellot, 35. Before Jonas Clarke accepted his job as minister, he demanded and received an outright payment of £133, an annual salary of £80, twenty cords of wood a year and the right to take additional wood from other citizens if necessary. *Ibid.*

[26] *Ibid*, 33.

[27] *Ibid*, 58.

[28] Anderson, 35.

be relied upon to wisely lead the community.[29] Between 1769
and 1779, twenty seven of the town's selectmen were between
the ages of fifty and fifty-nine. Another seventeen were
between the ages of forty and forty-nine. No one under the
age of thirty served as a selectman. Thus, dependent sons,
laborers, poor farmers and servants had no right to accept
leadership positions.[30]

Below the town politicians in the social order was the
general male population, or yeoman. Hard working and
dedicated to their beliefs, these men were concerned primarily
with raising their families and cultivating their farmlands. A
yeoman could vote in town elections and participate in town
meetings if he had resided in Lexington for one year, was at
least twenty-one years old and possessed an estate that would
rent for £3:6:8 a year according to the valuation of the local
assessor. As in many other towns, the average Lexington
farmer made up the rank and file of the militia. He could read,
generally refrained from drinking in excess, possessed high
moral standards and was often easily influenced by the Whig
propaganda emanating from Boston. His daily duties began at
dawn and continued, almost without interruption, until after
sunset.

A review of Lexington's tax valuations of property in
1774 reveals the wealthiest resident of Lexington, William
Reed, Esq., was assessed 16 shillings, one pence. The town's
poorest resident, Ephraim Winship, was assessed a mere ten
pence.[31] As such, most of the residents in Lexington were
considered "yeoman". The average Lexington yeoman

---

[29] *Ibid.*

[30] *Ibid.* Fuhrer, 90.

[31] Ibid. The decrease in many Lexington men's financial worth was due to
an increase in population prior to the war coupled with a fixed supply of
land available to inheriting sons. As a result, many young men in
Lexington were forced to seek land north or west of Lexington, purchase
smaller tracts of land inside Lexington or share with their brothers a
divided inheritance.

owned at least five cows, two oxen, at least six acres of tillage and produced at least sixty bushels of grain per year.[32]

Beneath the yeomen were the landless and poor. By 1774, nearly one third of Lexington men were landless. Many were young men, transients or non-inheriting sons who remained in town. More troubling was the number of poor who were dependent upon the town for support. In 1764, there were twelve individuals who were dependent upon the town. By 1775, the number doubled to twenty-four.[33] To curb the rise in government dependency, the town resolved to prosecute any resident who allowed nonresident poor to reside in their homes without first seeking permission of the selectmen. Fines assessed for conviction of minor misdemeanors were to be diverted to the support of the poor as was rotted and old wood found on town property.[34]

Popular belief to the contrary, slavery did exist in Massachusetts, and there were slaves living in Lexington at the outbreak of the Revolution.[35] In fact, slavery had existed in Massachusetts almost from its founding, but the institution had never flourished.[36] On the eve of the American Revolution, seven slaves resided in Lexington. The largest slave holder was Samuel Hadley with three servants.[37]

In some households, male slaves worked side by side with their masters as coopers, blacksmiths, shoemakers and wheelwrights. In other homes they ran errands, functioned as valets and performed heavy work for their masters. In Boston, slaves worked closely with sailors and merchants. The few female slaves in Lexington were required to carry out the

---

[32] http://sites.fas.harvard.edu/~hsb41/masstax/masstax.cgi.
[33] Fuhrer, 92.
[34] *Ibid.*
[35] The Massachusetts legislature legalized slavery in 1641.
[36] Anderson, 95.
[37] Slave holders in Lexington included Samuel Hadley with three slaves, Samuel Bridge with one slave, William Tidd with one slave, Robert Harrington with one slave and William Reed with one slave.

various household tasks their mistresses demanded.

Massachusetts slaves were not without rights. Unlike slaves in the southern colonies, New England slaves could hold property, serve in the militia (as was the case with five of Lexington's slaves: Prince Estabrook, Pompey Blackman, Samuel Crafts, Cato Tuder and Jupiter Tree) and testify in court against both whites and other blacks.[38] On rare occasions they were permitted to petition the colony for legal assistance. In 1774, several African-Americans addressed the Massachusetts General Court and demanded that they too have the right to enjoy the benefits of liberty. A slave could also sue for freedom, as was the case with a female mulatto slave named Margaret. On November 20, 1770, Margaret appeared in a court in Cambridge represented by a local Boston lawyer named Jonathan Sewall. John Adams, who was currently in the midst of the Boston Massacre trial, represented her masters, the Muzzey family of Lexington. At the end of the hearing, which lasted most of the day, the court freed Margaret.[39]

Still, slavery was a degrading and inhumane institution.[40] A slave could not move in search of opportunity or even travel outside of Lexington without the master's assent. If he were discovered, a slave would be prosecuted as a fugitive.[41] A slave could marry only with the master's

---

[38] However, it wasn't until the eve of the American Revolution that African-Americans were welcomed into the ranks of the militia. In 1652, the Massachusetts Legislature enacted a law requiring all African-Americans and Indian servants to undergo military training and serve in the militia. Four years later, fearing a slave revolt, Massachusetts reversed the law and prohibited African-Americans providing military service.

[39] Hiller Zobel, *Legal Papers of John Adams*, Vol. 2:50, 58-59 (1965)

[40] By 1667, most American colonies had recognized that a slave could not be freed from bondage by baptism, thereby discarding the Christian principle of enslaving other Christians. By 1667, the penalty for killing a slave was a mere £15.

[41] By 1643, all of the New England colonies had established laws punishing runaway slaves as "fugitives". In 1667, England enacted strict

blessing and interracial marriage was illegal. A slave's wife
and children could be sold to another owner at his master's
whim.[42]   Finally, a slave was always subject to both actual
and potential cruelty against which there was no defense. If a
slave struck a white man, he would be summarily and severely
punished.[43] On Boston Neck, travelers were presented with
the view of a cage containing the bones of Mark, a slave who
had been convicted of murdering his master. The spectacle
was intended to serve as a constant reminder to slaves in
Massachusetts of the potential penalties for defiance.[44]

  The women of Lexington occupied the bottom rung of
the social ladder. Prior to the war, most women were bound
by the legal and moral codes of their respective communities.
Life was not easy for women. From the perspective of
society, women were assumed to be helpless because they
were like children who could not provide the basic necessities
for themselves, but had to rely on men for food, shelter, and
clothing. But they were also helpless, it was thought, because
they were inferior. They could not take care of themselves
because they were less rational, capable, and competent than
men. Not only were women treated as helpless inferiors, they
were also expected to speak of themselves in these terms.[45]
Women in many of the colonies could not attend public
schools, were often pregnant on their wedding days and
received little protection from domestic violence.[46] Women

---

laws regulating slavery. A slave was forbidden to leave his master's
property without a pass or permission from his master and never on
Sunday.
[42] In 1670, the Massachusetts legislature passed a law permitting
slaveholders to sell children of slaves into bondage.
[43] By 1682, most American colonies prohibited self-defense by slaves.
[44] In 1700, a census report detailed over 27,000 enslaved people in the
American colonies. That same year, Chief Justice Samuel Sewall of the
Massachusetts Supreme Judicial Court published *The Selling of Joseph*, a
book outlining the economic and ethical grounds for abolishing slavery.
[45] Janice Potter McKinnon, *While the Women Only Wept*, (Montreal:
1993), 8.
[46] "The husband also (by the old law) might give his wife moderate

were often heavily dependent upon the companionship of their sisters and other female relatives. Siblings often spent countless hours spinning, preparing food, making soap and working in the field. Females also assisted each other in the birthing and raising of children.[47]

Often the major decision in a woman's life was the choice of a mate. Although 18th century women had some say in the selection of a spouse, parents still played a significant role in the decision and their consent was required.[48] Colonial era women were expected to obey their husbands, rear the children, cook and prepare meals, make and launder clothes and undertake minor household repairs.[49] A married woman was seen as subordinate to her husband. Basic to the marriage contract was the notion that the man had the power to make the important decisions for the family unit, but he also

---

correction. For, as he is to answer for her misbehaviour, the law thought it reasonable to intrust him with this power of restraining her, by domestic chastisement, in the same moderation that a man is allowed to correct his servants or children; for whom the master or parent is also liable in some cases to answer. But this power of correction was confined within reasonable bounds; and the husband was prohibited to use any violence to his wife, "[here translated:] other than as licitly and reasonably pertains to the husband for the rule and correction of his wife." The civil law gave the husband the same, or a larger, authority over his wife; allowing him, for some misdemesnors, "[here translated:] with flails and cudgels to beat the wife energetically;" for others, only "[here translated:] to apply limited punishment." But, with us, in the politer reign of Charles the second, this power of correction began to be doubted: and a wife may now have security of the peace against her husband; or, in return, a husband against his wife. Yet the lower rank of people, who were always fond of the old common law, still claim and exert their ancient privilege: and the courts of law will still permit a husband to restrain a wife of her liberty, in case of any gross misbehaviour." William Blackstone, *Commentaries on the Laws of England*, (London: 1765), 442-445.

[47] McKinnon, *While the Women*, 6.

[48] Ibid, 5.

[49] By comparison, a female camp follower in an 18th Century British regiment was considered an integral part of the organization. Most were gainfully employed as sutlers, nurses and laundresses, received financial compensation for their contributions and often had their own lodgings.

had the responsibility to ensure its well- being by providing the essentials - food, clothing, and housing.[50] Colonial era women were expected to obey their husbands, rear the children, cook and prepare meals, make and launder clothes and undertake minor household repairs.[51] Under the eyes of the law, a married woman could not vote, collect wages, make contracts, testify in court, serve as a juror, buy or sell property nor execute a will on her own. As eighteenth century legal scholar Sir William Blackstone surmised:

> By marriage, the husband and wife are one person in law: that is, the very being or legal existence of the woman is suspended during the marriage, or at least is incorporated and consolidated into that of the husband: under whose wing, protection, and *cover* she performs every thing; and is therefore called in our law-French a *feme-covert*; is said to be *covert-baron*, or under the protection and influence of her husband, her *baron*, or lord . . . [Though] our law in general considers man and wife as one person, yet there are some instances in which she is . . . considered; as inferior to him, and acting by his compulsion. And therefore all deeds executed, and acts done, by her . . . are void, or at least voidable; except it be a fine, or the like matter of record, in which case she must be solely and secretly examined, to learn if her act be voluntary. She cannot by will devise lands to her husband, unless under special circumstances; for at the time of making it she is supposed to be under his coercion. And in some felonies, and other inferior crimes, committed by her, though constraint of her husband, the law excuses her: but this extends not to treason or murder.[52]

---

[50] Ibid, 7.
[51] By comparison, a female camp follower in an 18th Century British regiment was considered an integral part of the organization. Most were gainfully employed as sutlers, nurses and laundresses, received financial compensation for their contributions and often had their own lodgings.
[52] Blackstone, *Commentaries*, 442-445.

Historical evidence suggests married colonial women, appeared to accept their subordinate position within the family. Rather than complaining or contemplating the unfairness of their situation, married women knew that their role was to accept their lot in life and do their duty. As loyalist Dothe Stone recalled "I was obliged and did affect cheerfulness in my behavior . . . I answered with a smile when my heart was ready to break. . . [I] must submit when it comes to open things."[53]

However, not all women were subject to the strict rigors of society. An unmarried woman was considered a *feme sole*. A *feme sole* could sign contracts, own a business, control her own wages, buy and/or sell property, and distribute personal property and chattel in her will. A *feme sole* could also sue or be sued in her own name in a court of law. Some *feme sole* loyalist women were able to establish employment as midwives, newspaper owners, successful seamstresses, tavern keepers, and shopkeepers. Such positions enabled women to work within the accepted sphere of gendered society (and/or sometimes in conjunction with family members, husbands, or business partners) and earn incomes that placed them in the middling ranks. For example, a Mrs. Cumming of Charlestown, South Carolina was a successful loyalist midwife who petitioned the British government for financial assistance following the loss of her business.[54] A Mrs. Griffiths, a Connecticut milliner, supported herself and her son prior to the war.[55] Unfortunately, the status of *feme*

---

[53] Dothe Stone, *Dothe Stone Diary, October 22, 1783*, Journal. From the Archives of Ontario, MS 519, reel 1; Ibid, October 24, 1783.
http://webcache.googleusercontent.com/search?q=cache:http://joelstone.ca/diary.html
[54] *American Loyalists, Transcripts of the Manuscript Books and Papers of the Commission of Enquiry into the Losses and Services of the American Loyalist*, IV, 284. From Robert Woodward Barnwell, Jr., "George Harland Hartle'ys Claim for Losses as a Loyalist," *The South Carolina Historical and Genealogical Magazine*, 51, no. 1 (1950): 45-50.
[55] Ibid,

sole afforded women the most freedom but was publicly and socially discouraged, since women were viewed as "unproductive" if they were not wedded and having babies.[56]

One limited way women established their rights during marriage and controlled their own businesses was to become *feme sole traders*. Most often, married women needed to obtain their husband's permission to do this. This status meant that married women could conduct business and were responsible for their own actions. If the women were sued, it would not affect their husbands' estates. Married women could even devise the property acquired through their own endeavors. Deserted women and sailors' wives could petition their colonial legislatures to acquire such status. Although not stated, it is easy to see that the legislatures granting such status acted in an effort to keep women and their dependent children off poor relief. Thus it was motivated by economic, rather than liberal, concerns. War would cause many women to support themselves because their husbands had died or were crippled as a result of their service. During most wars, women remained at home to run farms, plantations, and their families' businesses until the men returned from battle.

Women in the eighteenth century also acted independently as deputy husbands, a term coined by Laurel Thatcher Ulrich. As a deputy husband, the wife could take over her husband's job or business in his absence. This usually occurred in family businesses such as stores, taverns, mills, and the like. Women were familiar with the business and kept it running smoothly while their husbands were incapacitated or away. This role was common and women coped adequately with their new positions. The role of deputy husband allowed married women to purchase supplies, pay bills, bank, and

---

[56] If a young woman did not marry, she was expected to live with her brother, or some other married male relative, and help care for his family. The male relative would assume the responsibility of caretaker and provider for the single woman.

perform all other aspects of running their businesses. During times of war, women ran their plantations, businesses, farms, families, and managed the servants, while their husbands served in the military. Such was the case during the American Revolution and women, whether Tory or Whig, did whatever was necessary to keep the home front running.

Many colonial women, whether Loyalist or Patriot, were forced during the Revolution to act in ways inconsistent with their subordinate status within patriarchal households and to take their first tentative steps into the traditionally male-dominated worlds of politics and war fare. Loyalist women were active participants in the Revolution. They took their first steps into the political realm by petitioning and writing pamphlets. In one such piece of literature, Abigail Adams to opine to her husband John on the eve of the Declaration of Independence

> I long to hear that you have declared an independency -- and by the way in the new Code of Laws which I suppose it will be necessary for you to make I desire you would Remember the Ladies, and be more generous and favourable to them than your ancestors. Do not put such unlimited power into the hands of the Husbands. Remember all Men would be tyrants if they could. If perticuliar care and attention is not paid to the Laidies we are determined to foment a Rebelion, and will not hold ourselves bound by any Laws in which we have no voice, or Representation. That your Sex are Naturally Tyrannical is a Truth so thoroughly established as to admit of no dispute, but such of you as wish to be happy willingly give up the harsh title of Master for the more tender and endearing one of Friend. Why then, not put it out of the power of the vicious and the Lawless to use us with cruelty and indignity with impunity. Men of Sense in all Ages abhor those customs which treat us only as the vassals of your Sex. Regard us then as Beings placed by

providence under your protection and in immitation of the Supreem Being make use of that power only for our happiness.[57]

---

[57] Letter from Abigail Adams to John Adams, March 31, 1776.

~2~

An Appeal to Heaven

Religion in the 17th and 18th centuries was part of the very lifeblood of Lexington. From the establishment of Cambridge Farms to the arrival of the Reverend John Hancock in 1698, Lexington citizens subscribed to the Calvinist theory of Puritanism. The origins of Puritanism can be traced back to England where the movement was an attempt to continue the Protestant Reformation by further purifying the Church of England. The spread of Puritanism in England received a temporary check when, under Charles I, the Declaration of 1628 named the king as the supreme leader of the church. The government then imposed immediate restrictions on Puritan sermons and publications, and began to imprison those who ignored the injunctions. Twenty thousand Puritans, rather than submit to these restrictions, chose to leave England, eventually arriving in New England, where they established their "Church in the Wilderness."

Following the execution of Charles I at the end of the English Civil War, Oliver Cromwell rose to power. Under Cromwell's "Protectorate," Puritans gained another temporary reprieve, and the freedom to practice their beliefs. However, with Cromwell's death, and the restoration of the monarchy under Charles II, persecution of Puritans resumed. Those responsible for the execution of Charles I were pursued and executed, and those who continued to espouse the Puritan doctrine were once again forced to choose between emigration or continued persecution in England. As a result, a second wave of Puritans left England and fled to New England, where they were free to openly express their theological beliefs.

In the midst of this "Church in the Wildernes" was Lexington. Its residents, like most of the Massachusetts Bay colonists, adhered to a strict form of Calvinism characterized by a vengeful Jehovah and ministers imposing the laws of Christ upon their flocks.[58] Parishioners were required to submit themselves to the authority of the local minister and could only become full members within the church if they entered into a personal "covenant" with God.[59] Membership was restricted to those elite who could demonstrate to the minister and a panel of select parishioners God's presence in their lives.[60] It was this privileged group who were admitted to the Lord's Supper and who oversaw the business of the church.[61]

In the aftermath of the Salem Witch Trials, however, the religious fervor of Lexington waned. Church membership dwindled as fewer residents stepped forward to proclaim their covenant with God. But with the rise of the "Great Awakening" in the 1740s, "New Lights" welcomed the energetic and emotional sermons of popular ministers. Likewise, laymen were allowed to preach from the pulpit. Ministers from other towns and parishes were invited to speak, with morality becoming the underlying theme of many sermons. Emotion and extravagant gestures replaced solemn hymns and prayers. Lexington residents were instructed to judge and interpret the laws of Christ on their own.

---

[58] Tourtellot, 39, 41.

[59] *Ibid*, 40.

[60] Gross, 19.

[61] This included joining with the town in hiring a minister.

Many Lexington residents rejected the followings of "Old Lights". From the perspective of New Lights, the privileges of elites, the restrictive religious ceremonies and selective church membership were considered offensive and contrary to church doctrine. In short, the Old Lights were viewed as heretics and enemies of the congregation.

Reverend Hancock recognized that the Great Awakening could create a split in his congregation; as it did in Concord and other communities. Rather than drive a wedge through the members of his church, Hancock adopted a position of compromise during the height of the Great Awakening. On the one hand Hancock found the emotional practices of the New Lights unacceptable and troubling. On the other hand, the reverend took advantage of the religious awakening to draw in new members. During his tenure, Lexington's minister encouraged individual thought, freedom of conscious and community piety. Hancock even went as far as to encourage the adoption of a choir and singing of Isaac Watt's hymns. During his tenure, the Reverend Hancock successfully drew in over eighty new church members.

Hancock and Clarke even endorsed the concept of a "halfway covenant," whereby those who could not provide the evidence necessary to prove their covenant with God in order to become full members of the church could still enjoy some of the benefits and privileges of membership.[62]

Despite this "liberal" approach to religion, the basic tenants of Puritanism remained intact in Lexington. Well into the era of the French and Indian War, men still adhered to the belief that the Lord directly interposed his hand in worldly affairs in order to implement his eternal plan of salvation. This providential concept of reality had profound impact on the expectations of New Englanders. In their minds, God visited both blessings and chastisement upon those who he

---

[62] Such benefits included baptizing children and participation in church services.

loved. He rewarded those deserving of reward, but expected them in turn to offer thanksgiving for his blessings.[63] Conversely, God punished those who deserved punishment. And those who failed to acknowledge the Lord's workings, or even worse, committed the sin of pride, would feel the wrath of God. Diaries and journals of Massachusetts provincial soldiers during the French and Indian War were filled with references to the Lord's disciplinary actions. Included among these chastisements were freak weather storms, disease and starvation, accidental death and finally, defeat in battle.[64] Most New Englanders believed that it was only through the Lord's workings that a collective effort such as war could succeed. Unless the group as a whole conformed to His purpose, none were of use to Him.

The idea of "liberty" was an important component of Puritan theology. However, an individual's liberty depended not on his financial circumstances, but rather upon his moral character. Real and substantial liberties were to be sought from within rather than from outside sources. Liberty was related to sobriety of conduct and integrity of life. Liberty was ordered, just as life was ordered. To obtain freedom, one was expected to both strive individually and work cooperatively within the community. The divine lesson was to obey God and then through the firm, collective obedience of all individuals, liberty could be attained. [65]

On the eve of the American Revolution, the unique position of the minister within Lexington guaranteed that Clarke would play a significant role in the unfolding political drama. When the Revolutionary crisis began in 1765, the

---

[63] Anderson, 198.
[64] For further examples of Providentialism during the French and Indian War: *Journal of Seth Metcal*, April 25, 1757, December 30, 1795; *Journal of Joseph Nichols*, June 6, 1758, June 8, 1758, June 24, 1758, August 9, 1758, September 3, 1758; *Journal of Caleb Rea*, July 10, 1758.
[65] David Hackett Fischer, *Paul Revere's Ride*, (New York, New York: Oxford University Press, 1994), xvii.

Reverend Clarke, already the community's spiritual leader, quickly emerged as its political leader as well, and the voice of Lexington's opposition to British policy.

Through his skilled diagnosis of the issues, Jonas Clarke ensured Lexington's unity against England. He gradually drew the townspeople into a national debate and accustomed them to the idea and practice of acting on a broad political stage that extended beyond mere town affairs. His influence shaped attitudes and molded public opinion. During his tenure in Lexington, his sermons included such themes as "The Importance of Military Skill", "Measures for Defense", "A Marshall Spirit in a Time of Peace" and "The Fate of Blood". Each time Parliament passed a series of new acts affecting the colonies, Jonas Clarke wrote long, closely reasoned responses that were quickly adopted and endorsed by the citizens of Lexington at their town meetings. When the Stamp Act crisis arose, he called it a "door to numberless evils, which only time can discover."[66] In 1768, he condemned the quartering of troops in the colonies as "an infringement of their natural, constitutional and chartered rights."[67] In 1773, following the passage of a tea tax, Jonas Clarke argued that any Lexington citizen who purchased or consumed tea "should be looked upon as an enemy of the town . . . and shall . . . be treated with neglect and contempt."[68] When the Intolerable Acts were passed, Lexington concluded, under the guidance of Clarke, that the time had come to prepare for war.[69] Quickly, the town's resolve was voiced: "We shall be ready to sacrifice our estates and everything dear in life, yea and life itself, in support of the common cause."[70]

---

[66] "Instructions from Jonas Clarke to William Reed Esq., the Present Representative of Lexington, October 21, 1765."

[67] Declarations and Resolves, Town of Lexington, September 21, 1768.

[68] Report of the Committee of Correspondence adopted by the Town of Lexington, December 1773.

[69] Tourtellot, 45.

[70] Report of the Committee of Correspondence adopted by the Town of Lexington, December 1773.

New England's Puritans had always considered the state's defense of Protestantism as essential to their prized English liberties.[71] Recognizing this principle, Clarke carefully linked English rights and liberties to theology. Clarke saw the colonists of Massachusetts Bay Colony as Chosen People who were tasked with the responsibility of reestablishing Israel's purity of worship and moral authority. Thus, the people of Massachusetts were required to defend their Chosen Land. As Clarke declared in 1768 "the preservation of the rights and liberties of the people [was in fact] the cause of GOD... Militiamen who engage in the cause of [God's] people, and set themselves for their defense, are therefore to consider themselves as guardians and trustees for GOD, having the rights, property, liberties, and lives of their fellow-men (a sacred trust!),committed to their charge."[72]

Initially Clarke's arguments to his people relied heavily upon the rights of Englishmen set forth in the Magna Carte and the Massachusetts Provincial Charter of 1690.[73] In 1763, Clarke wrote "We shall have and enjoy all Liberties and Immunities of Free and Natural Subjects within any of his Majesties Dominions . . . as if we were every one of us born in his Majesties Realm in England."[74] As the years passed and grievances mounted, Clarke began to lay the groundwork for an assertion of rights independent of those granted by the Crown. As the Massachusetts assembly defied British ultimatums, some provincials, including Clarke, held that Crown and parliamentary powers were not without limit. Drawing on Enlightenment philosophy, he contended that "in a state of

---

[71] Fuhrer, 106.
[72] Jonas Clarke, *The Importance of Military Skill, Measures for Defense and a Martial Spirit, in a Time of Peace: A Sermon Preached to the Ancient and Honorable Artillery Company in Boston, New-England, June 6, 1768 Being the Anniversary of their Election of Officers* (Boston: Kneeland and Adams, 1768), pp. 15–16.
[73] Fuhrer, 107.
[74] Instructions to Representative to General Court, William Reed, Esq., Lexington Town Meeting Records, 21 October 1765

nature, every man has a right to liberty, property and life: And no one . . . can, reasonably, deprive him of either. Society is formed for the preservation and defense of the common rights of mankind, to that end, that the blessings of life may be secured to all. The liberties and privileges, the property and possessions of society, ought always to be held sacred; and no one is at liberty to invade, violate, or even incroach upon them, upon any pretence whatsoever."[75]

Through his tireless efforts, Clarke not only created a political climate in Lexington that was well ahead of most Massachusetts towns, he also influenced the public opinions of many other clergymen and statesmen within the colony as well.[76] On the eve of the Battle of Lexington, Clarke often journeyed outside of Lexington to neighboring communities and Boston to give guest sermons, attend political rallies, offer lectures and observe business matters. Clarke became so popular he was frequently asked to serve as a guest speaker at clergy ordinations. In fact, so many of the clergy followed Clark's example that by the eve of the Battles of Lexington and Concord, General Hugh Earl Percy put forward the following complaint in a letter to his father. "I am sorry to say that no body of men in this Province are so extremely injurious to the peace and tranquility of it as the clergy. They preach sedition openly from their pulpits. (Nay, some of them have gone so far as absolutely to refuse the sacrament to the communicants till they have signed a paper of the most seditious kind, which they have denominated the Solemn League and Covenant). So much with respect to the inhabitants."[77]

As the Lexington militia anxiously awaited the approach of the regulars in the early morning of April 19, 1775, the Reverend Clarke was confident he had adequately prepared his people for the coming conflict. As Clarke had

---

[75] Fuhrer, 107.
[76] Tourtellot, 44.
[77] Letter from Percy to the Duke of Northumberland, July 27, 1774.

forewarned a little over a year earlier in January, 1774, "Our worthy ancestors after many struggles with their enemies, in the face of every danger, and at the expense of much treasure & bloode, secured to themselves & transmitted to us their posterity a fair and rich inheritance, not only of a pleasant & fertile lande but also of invaluable rights & privileges both as men & christians. . . . We looke upon ourselves as bounde by the most sacred ties to the utmost of our power to maintain, and defende ourselves, in our charter Rights and privileges, and as a sacred trust committed to us to transmit them, inviolate, to succeeding generations."[78]

---

[78] Lexington Town Meeting Records, 5 January 1774.

~3~

The Plan of Oppression: Lexington on the Eve of the American Revolution

The origins of the American Revolution can be traced back to the close of the French and Indian War (1754-1763). Following its conquest of Canada, England began to recognize the harsh realities of its victory. In the months following the Treaty of Paris, Great Britain was forced not just to administer its newly acquired territories, but also to defend them. This necessitated maintaining a ten thousand-man army to protect North America from future French operations and Native American attacks, such as Pontiac's Rebellion, which ignited after the conclusion of the war. By January 5, 1763, Britain's funded debt was a staggering £122,603,336 with an annual interest of £4,409,797. A year later, the debt was almost £7,000,000 larger and by January of 1767, it had increased yet another £7,000,000.[79]

In an attempt to curb this financial burden, the English government implemented a series of economic programs

---

[79] Robert MiddleKauff, *The Glorious Cause: The American Revolution, 1763 - 1789*, (New York, New York: Oxford University Press, 1982), 57.

aimed at having those it considered to have benefited most by the successful conclusion of the war, the American colonies, share in the burden of debt. After reviewing the state of Britain's finances, Chancellor of Exchequer, George Grenville, concluded that the American colonies had benefited greatly from the protection of the Crown while contributing very little in taxes. At the same time, Grenville pointed out, an active smuggling trade coupled with massive colonial customs mismanagement, particularly in the New England region, had led to an annual £6,000 deficit in custom duties collected in American ports. Accordingly, he suggested that a direct tax be levied on the American colonies in order to generate additional revenue.[80]

The first two revenue raising measures that Great Britain imposed on her American colonies were the Sugar Act of 1764 and the Stamp Act of 1765. The Sugar Act established tariffs on colonial trading and also attempted to curb the American practice of smuggling sugar and molasses from the West Indies by placing a three pence per gallon tax on foreign molasses. The act established a list of "enumerated goods" that could be shipped only to England, including lumber, and set forth procedures for the accounting, loading and unloading of cargo in port. Violations of the act were prosecuted in a vice admiralty court, where defendants would be denied the right to a jury trial and where the presumption was of guilt rather than innocence. The second revenue raising measure was the Stamp Act, which levied an unprecedented direct tax on almost every piece of public paper in the colonies. Newspapers, almanacs, deeds, wills, custom documents, even playing cards were among the many papers subjected to the tax. The Stamp Act went so far as to impose a tax upon *tax receipts*.

The Sugar and Stamp acts brought on an explosion of

---

[80] Grenville also established reforms in the way custom duties were collected and accounted.

riots, boycotts and protests throughout the colonies, particularly in Massachusetts. At first, Massachusetts' response was peaceful, with the inhabitants merely boycotting certain goods. However, resistance to the taxes soon became more violent. Under the guidance of Samuel Adams, Bostonians began a campaign of terror directed against those who supported the Stamp Act. It began on August 14, 1765 with an effigy of Andrew Oliver, the appointed stamp distributor for Massachusetts, being hung from a "liberty tree" in plain view by the "sons of liberty." That evening, the Oliver's luxurious home was burned to the ground. A chastened Oliver quickly resigned his commission. The following evening, incited by a rumor that he supported the Stamp Act, the home of Thomas Hutchinson, Lieutenant Governor of the colony, was surrounded by an unruly mob. When Hutchinson refused to accede to the demand that he come out and explain his position, the mob broke several windows and then dispersed. Two weeks later, on August 28, 1765, an even larger mob assembled and descended upon the homes of several individuals suspected of favoring the Stamp Act, including again that of the Lieutenant Governor. Hutchinson managed to evacuate his family to safety before the mob arrived. Then, as Hutchinson later described it, "the hellish crew fell upon my house with the rage of divels and in a moment with axes split down the door and entered. My son heard them cry 'damn him he is upstairs we'll have him.' Some ran immediately as high as the top of the house, others filled the rooms below and cellars and others remained without the house to be employed there. I was obliged to retire thro yards and gardens to a house more remote where I remained until 4 o'clock by which time one of the best finished houses in the Province had nothing remaining but the bare walls and floors."[81]

The mob's show of force had the desired effect. With Oliver's resignation, the stamps could not be properly

---

[81] Hutchinson to Richard Jackson, August 30, 1765.

distributed. Additionally, no other stamp officer was willing to step forward to assume Oliver's legal role. In short, Boston was crippled and could not enforce the act. The town standoff between Boston and the Crown continued through the fall and winter of 1765.

Lexington, being both close in proximity and tied economically to Boston, quickly became embroiled in the stamp crisis. A town meeting was held on October 21, 1765 to address the Stamp question, and determine what instructions should be given to William Reed, the representative of Lexington to the Massachusetts General Court. A committee was established, composed of the selectmen James Stone, Thaddeus Bowman, Robert Harrington, Benjamin Brown and Samuel Stone, Jr. Supervised by the Reverend Clarke, the committee drafted a series of instructions. Although stopping short of challenging Parliament's right to pass laws regulating the American colonies, the instructions from Lexington did challenge the perceived results of the act:

> What of all most alarms Us is an Act Commonly Called the Stamp Act, the full Execution of which we Apprehend would divest us of our Most inestimable Charter Rights and Privileges, Rob us of our Character as Free and Natural Subjects, and of almost Everything we ought as a People hold Dear. Admitting that there was No Dispute as to the Right of Parliament to impose such an Act upon us, yet we Cannot forbear Complaining of it in itself considered, as unequal and unjust, and a Yoke too heavy for us to bear, And that not only as it falls heaviest on the poor, the widow and the fatherless and the orphan, not only will it embarrass the Trade and Business of this infant country . . . But more especially . . . it will quickly drein the Country of little Cash remaining in it, Strip

---

[82] Declarations and Resolves, Town of Lexington, October 21, 1765.

Multitudes of their Property and reduce them to Poverty.[82]

The committee further asserted that the act was in violation of the basic rights and liberties guaranteed to them as Englishmen, an opinion shared by many of the residents of Massachusetts. The prevailing view in Massachusetts during this crisis was that the power to tax rested not with Parliament, but with the colony's General Court. Invoking the colony's Royal Charter and the right to self-government guaranteed therein, the committee declared

> We humbly conceive this Act to be directly repugnant to those Rights and Privileges granted to us in our Charter, which we always hold sacred, as confirmed to us by the Royal word and Seal, and as frequently recognized by our Sovereign and the Parliament of Great Britain, wherein it is expressly granted to us and to our children--- That We shall have and enjoy all Liberties and Immunities of Free and Natural Subjects, within any of His Majesty's Dominions, to all intents, and . . . Further, that the Full Power and Authority to impose and levy proportionable and reasonable Taxes, upon the Estates and Persons of all the Inhabitants within the Province, for the Support and Defense of His Majesty's Government, are granted to the [Massachusetts] General Court or Assembly thereof.

> But by this Act a Tax, ---Yea, a heavy Tax, is imposed, Not only without and beside the Authority of Said General Court, in which this power, (which has never been forfeited nor be given up) is Said to be Fully and exclusively lodged; But also directly in opposition to an essential Right or Privilege of Free and Natural Subjects of Great Britain, who look upon it as their Darling and Constitutional Right never to be Taxed but by their own Consent, in Person or by their

---

[83] *Ibid.*

Representatives.[83]

The resolution also chastised Parliament for its decision to eliminate the right to a jury trial by transferring prosecutions to admiralty courts. "By this Act we are most deeply affected as hereby we are debarred of being tried by juries in case of any breach or supposed breach of it, - a right which, until now, we have held in common with our brethren in England . . . This we apprehend will open a door to numberless evils which time only can discover."[84]

Yet, Lexington was not Boston. The citizens of the small dairy town rejected the use of violence and rioting. The town resolutions even went to great lengths to "earnestly recommend to [William Reed] the most calm, decent and dispassionate measures for our open, explicit and resolute assertion and vindication of our charter rights and liberties . . . We take it for granted, therefore, that you will carefully avoid all unaccustomed and unconstitutional grants, which will not only add to the present burden, but make such precedents as will be attended with consequences which may prove greatly to the disadvantage of the public."[85]

With the riots receiving widespread coverage in London newspapers coupled with the successful boycott program undertaken by New York, Philadelphia and Boston, England finally yielded. Realizing the Stamp and Sugar Acts could never be enforced in America, the acts were repealed on March 4, 1766. However, before striking the laws, Parliament announced the Declaratory Act of 1766, which emphasized its authority to legislate for the colonies in all cases whatsoever.

It was not long before the members of the Parliament made use of the principle expressed in the Declaratory Act. 1767 faced England with a projected annual cost of almost £400,000 to maintain her army in America. Charles

---

[84] *Ibid.*
[85] *Ibid.*

Townshend, the impetuous Chancellor of the Exchequer, of whom it was said, "his mouth often outran his mind", suddenly announced that he knew how to tax the American colonies. This so pleased the House of Commons that they promptly voted to lower English land taxes from four shillings on the pound to three, resulting in a £500,000 loss of revenue and threatening fiscal chaos. To meet this crisis, Townshend suggested, and Parliament enacted, a series of laws directed at raising revenue from the American colonies. The Townshend Acts, as they became known, provided for an American import tax on paper, painter's lead, glass and tea. The acts also tightened custom policies and revived the vice-admiralty courts. Although a minority within the House of Commons opposed such a measure, the majority rationalized it would "raise colonial revenue, punish the colonists for their ill-behavior after the repeal of the Stamp Act, and exercise the rights to which Parliament laid claim in the Declaratory Act."[86]

Once again, Boston stood at the forefront of opposition. On October 28, 1767, the citizens resolved, at a town meeting, to oppose the acts by refusing to import English goods and to encourage American manufacture instead. Lexington followed Boston's initiative. On December 28, 1767, Lexington "Voted unanimously, to concur with the town of Boston respecting importing and using foreign commodities, as mentioned in their votes, passed at their meeting on the twenty-eighth day of October, 1767."[87]

However, by 1768, Boston was once again resorting to violence to indicate its opposition to British policy. In March, rioters went to "Commissioner Burch's home and with clubs assembled before his door a great part of the evening, and he was obliged to send away his wife and children by a back door."[88] Inspector William Woolton returned home one evening to find "4 men passing him, one with a stick or

---

[86] Zobel, 62.
[87] Declarations and Resolves, Town of Lexington, December 28, 1767.
[88] Letter from Bernard to Shelburne, March 19, 1768.

42

bludgeon in his hand accosted him saying, 'Damn your Blood
we will be at you to Morrow night."[89] The victims of the mob
begged Governor Bernard to apply for military protection so
the Townshend Acts could be enforced. The governor
struggled with the decision, but ultimately applied to the king
for troops. At the same time, however, British merchants
pleaded with Parliament and the King to repeal the act before
they were brought to financial ruin. Yet their pleas went
unanswered. In 1768, Governor Bernard was ordered to
dissolve the Massachusetts legislature, and two full regiments
of British regulars were dispatched to Boston to protect the
custom officials and help to enforce the Townsend Acts.

Lexington's inhabitants reacted with dismay. On
September 21, 1768, they assembled "to take into their serious
consideration the distressed state of the Province at the present
day, and to pass any vote thereto."[90] Isaac Bowman, William
Reed, Esq., and Deacon James Stone were selected "to prepare
reasons for our present conduct."[91] After much consideration,
the three men presented a series of resolves to the town. The
resolves looked for precedent to the act passed by Parliament
during the first year of the reign of William and Mary, settling
the succession of the crown and declaring the rights and
liberties of their subjects. In particular, they appealed to the
Massachusetts Royal Charter, for the authority to forthrightly
defend their rights as Englishmen. The residents of
Lexington, through their resolves, argued that it was explicitly
stated in the charter of Massachusetts that as inhabitants of the
colony they possessed

Certain rights, Liberties & privileges therein Expressly
mentioned: Among which it is Granted, Established
and ordained That all and every ye Subjects of Them,
their heirs and Successors, which Shall Go to inhabit
within Sd Province & territory, & Every of their

---

[89] Deposition of William Woolton, March 18, 1768.
[90] Declarations and Resolves, Town of Lexington, September 21, 1768.
[91] *Ibid.*

children which shall happen to be born there . . . Shall
have & injoy all the Liberties and Immunities of free &
Natural Subjects . . .as if they & every of them were
Born within the Realm of England."[92]

As was the practice at this time, the people of
Lexington acknowledged "their firm & unshaken allegiance to
their alone rightful Sovereign King George the Third,"[93]
However, they went on to assert:

> [That] the freeholders & other Inhabitants of the Town
> of Lexington will, at the utmost peril of their Lives and
> Fortunes, take all Legal and Constitutional measures to
> Defend and maintain ye person, Family, Crown and
> Dignity of our Said Sovereign Lord, George ye Third,
> and all and Singular the Rights, Liberties, privileges
> and Immunities Granted in said Royal Charter as well
> as those which are Declared to be Belonging to us as
> British subjects, by Birthright as all others therein
> Specially mentioned.[94]

The resolves concluded by condemning as
infringement of the Royal Charter both the policy of levying
taxes without consent of the people of Massachusetts or their
elected representative, and the quartering of troops in Boston.

> Therefore, Voted as ye opinion of this Town, that
> levying money within this Province for the Use and
> Service of ye Crown in other manner than ye same is
> Granted by the Great and General Court or Assembly
> of this province is in violation of ye Said Royal
> Charter: and . . .the Raising & keeping a Standing
> Army among them . . . without their consent in person
> or by representatives of their own free Election, would
> be an Infringement of their Natural, Constitutional and

---

[92] *Ibid.*
[93] *Ibid.*
[94] *Ibid.*

Charter rights.[95]

The resolves of 1768 represented a departure from the town's earlier position as stated during the Stamp Act crisis. Gone was the tone of deferential disagreement, along with the expressed desire to avoid the violence that had plagued Boston. No longer was the argument focused primarily on the economic impact of British taxation policies. Although stopping short of justifying a resort to arms, the 1768 resolves demonstrated the town's unwavering devotion to their constitutional rights and its willingness to defend those liberties at all costs within *legal bounds*. The residents noticed the change in tone as well. The report was debated and read several times before it was finally accepted with a unanimous vote. Still, Lexington knew they had taken a momentous step and now could not turn back. At the conclusion of the town meeting, they voted "to keep a day of prayer on the occasion, and left to the Rev. Mr. Clarke to appoint the time."[96]

Following the Lexington resolves, the town also adopted a boycott of all British goods. Women organized spinning bees to decrease dependence on imports. As the *Boston Gazette* observed on August 31, 1769 "very early in the morning, the young Ladies of [Lexington], to the number of 45, assembled at the house of Mr. Daniel Harrington, with their Spinning Wheels, where they spent the day in the most pleasing satisfaction: and at night presented Mrs. Harrington with the spinning of 602 knots of linen and 346 knots of cotton. If any should be inclin'd to treat such assemblies or the publication of them in a contemptuous sneer as thinking them quite ludicrous, such persons would do well first to consider what would become of one of our (so much boasted) manufactures, on which we pretend the welfare our country is so much depending, if those of the fair sex

---

[95] *Ibid.*
[96] *Ibid.*

should refuse to "lay their hands to the spindle" or be unwilling to "hold the distaff." Prov. 31:19."[97]

Instead of reestablishing law and order, the Townsend Acts only provoked further violence. On March 5, 1770, an angry mob began to badger and taunt a lone British sentry on guard duty in front of the Boston Custom House. When the crowd began to pelt him with snowballs, ice and other objects, he called for help and was reinforced by a squad of soldiers from the 29th Regiment of Foot. The crowd pressed closer, and the nervous regulars opened fire. Five men in the crowd were killed and a number of others were wounded. The soldiers were arrested, tried and all but two were acquitted.[98] The Boston Massacre, as the incident became known, sparked widespread outrage and pushed the colonies dangerously close to rebellion. To forestall an uprising, Parliament again retreated, repealing all the Townsend Acts, except a symbolic tax on tea of which no immediate attempt was made to collect.[99]

However, in 1773, Parliament passed the Tea Act in an attempt to finally collect the tax on tea, and to refinance the shaky economic base of the British East India Company.

---

[97] *Boston Gazette and Country Journal*, 16 October 1769.

[98] Two soldiers were found guilty of manslaughter, branded on their thumbs and then released.

[99] For the next two years, tensions seemed to lessen in the colonies, particularly Massachusetts. However, when Parliament attempted to control provincial judges in 1772 by directly controlling their salaries, Massachusetts quickly responded in opposition and protest. On January 5, 1773, Lexington joined with other towns and "voted, also, that this town has a right to correspond with other towns upon matters of common concern, and that a Committee be accordingly chosen to transmit the proceeding of this meeting to the Gentlemen of the Committee of Correspondence in Boston; and, further, to correspond with them, as well as the committee of other towns, upon matters of common concern, as occasions may require." The town chose Captain Thaddeus Bowman, Jonas Stone, Ensign Robert Harrington, Benjamin Brown and Joseph Loring to serve on the committee. Declarations and Resolves, Town of Lexington, January 5, 1773.

Established in 1709, the East India Company derived over ninety-percent of its profits from the sale of tea. However, by 1772, due to severe mismanagement, the company was in desperate need of a bailout. The company directors looked to Parliament for relief. Parliament's response was the Tea Act, through which the East India Company was given exclusive rights to ship tea to America without paying import duties and to sell it through their agents to American retailers. American merchants who had for years purchased tea from non-British sources (Dutch tea was a particular favorite of New Englanders) faced the prospect of financial ruin.

Massachusetts immediately opposed the act and began to organize resistance. On November 29, 1773, the tea ship *Dartmouth* arrived at Griffin's Wharf in Boston. Three days later, the *Beaver* and the *Eleanor* arrived at the same wharf. Bostonians demanded that Governor Hutchinson order the three ships back to England. On December 16, 1773, the owner of the *Dartmouth* apparently agreed and went to Hutchinson to beg him to let the ships return to England. Hutchinson refused, and at approximately six o'clock that evening, some 150 men and boys disguised as Indians marched to the three ships, boarded them and dumped 340 chests of tea into Boston Harbor.

Meanwhile, as tempers boiled over in Boston, the citizens of Lexington assembled three days *prior* to the Boston Tea Party to discuss the unfolding events. The matter was referred to the town's committee of correspondence, which quickly drafted an emotional and stinging condemnation of the Tea Act.

> [It] appears that the Enemies of the Rights & Liberties of Americans, greatly disappointed in the Success of the Revenue Act, are seeking to Avail themselves of New, & if possible, Yet more detestable Measures to distress, Enslave & destroy us. Not enough that a Tax was laid Upon Teas, which should be Imported by Us,

for the Sole Purpose of Raising a revenue to support Taskmasters, Pensioners, &c., in Idleness and Luxury; But by a late Act of Parliament, to Appease the wrath of the East India Company, whose Trade to America had been greatly clogged by the operation of the Revenue Acts, Provision is made for said Company to export their teas to America free and discharged from all Duties and Customs in England, but liable to all the same Rules, Regulations, Penalties & Forfeitures in America, as are Provided by the Revenue Act . . . Not to say anything of the Gross Partiality herein discovered in favour of the East India Company, and to the Injury & oppression of Americans; . . . we are most especially alarmed, as by these Crafty Measures of the Revenue Act is to be Established, and the Rights and Liberties of Americans forever Sapped & destroyed. These appear to Us to be Sacrifices we must make, and these the costly Pledges that must be given Up into the hands of the Oppressor. The moment we receive this detested Article, the Tribute will be established upon   Us . . . Once admit this subtle, wicked Ministerial Plan to take place, once permit this Tea . . . to be landed, received and vended . . . the Badge of our slavery is fixed, the Foundation of ruin is surely laid.[100]

The committee also issued six resolves pledging to preserve and protect the constitutional rights that Parliament had put into jeopardy, to boycott any teas "sent out by the East India Company, or that shall be imported subject to a duty imposed by Act of Parliament,"[101] to treat as enemies anyone found aiding in the landing, selling or using of tea from the East India Company, and to treat the merchants of the East India Company with contempt. Finally, the town expressed its

---

[100] Report of the Committee of Correspondence adopted by the Town of Lexington, December 1773.
[101] *Ibid.*

gratitude to Boston for its undertaking in the name of liberty, and pledged

> We are ready and resolved to concur with them in every rationale Measure that may be Necessary for the Preservation or Recovery of our Rights and Liberties as Englishmen and Christians; and we trust in God That, should the State of Our Affairs require it, We shall be ready to Sacrifice our Estates and everything dear in Life, Yea and Life itself, in support of the common Cause.[102]

Upon completion, the Town of Lexington with a unanimous vote adopted the resolves. Immediately afterwards, an additional resolve was passed, warning the residents

> That if any Head of a Family in this Town, or any Person, shall from this time forward; & until the Duty taken off, purchase any Tea, Use or consume any Tea in their Famelies [sic], such person shall be looked upon as an Enemy to this town & to this Country, and shall by this Town be treated with Neglect & Contempt.[103]

That evening, the residents of Lexington gathered all tea supplies and burned them. "We are positively informed that the patriotic inhabitants of Lexington unanimously resolved against against the use of Bohea tea of all sorts, Dutch or English importation; and to manifest the sincerity of their resolution, they brought together every ounce contained in the town, and committed it to one common bonfire."[104]

The resolves of Lexington reflected the general political mood throughout the American colonies on the eve of

---

[102] *Ibid.*

[103] *Ibid.*

[104] *Massachusetts Spy*, December 16, 1773.

the revolution. Many colonists believed a set of corrupt and mysterious men had been able to assert control over George the Third, his ministers and his favorites through bribery and deceit. Most Americans were certain that powerful men were plotting to make the colonists slaves by curtailing their liberties as Englishmen.

The common belief emerged that an immoral British government, having exhausted opportunities for plunder and profit in England and Ireland, was now seeking a dispute with the American colonies as an excuse to enslave and deprive them of their wealth and liberties. Parliament had hoped to accomplish this goal quietly, but the furor aroused in the colonies by England's economic policies had given the government a temporary setback. Now, these mysterious men, who controlled Parliament and the king's ministers, were undertaking to openly incite a war, declare American rebels and enslave them. As early as 1772, Lexington was expressing apprehension that

> [Our] Charter Rights & Liberties are in danger, are infringed and upon a most careful, Serious & mature Consideration of them . . . and are comparing them with Acts of the British Parliament, & Measures adopted by the British Court, Ministry & Government . . .some of which have been carried into Execution amongst us, We are clearly of opinion that . . . the Plan of Oppression is begun, & so far carried on that, if our Enemies are still Successful, and no Means can be found to put a Stop to their Career, . . . we have just Reason to fear That the Eyes of the Head of Government being blinded, the Sources of Justice poisoned and Hands of administration bribed with interest, the system of slavery will soon be compleat.[105]

The colonists concerns and fears so evident in letters,

---

[105] Declarations and Resolves, Town of Lexington, January 5, 1773.

journals, and diaries of the period increased following the Boston Tea Party. That action was viewed in England as so rebellious an act of defiance that it could not be ignored. As a result, the English Parliament adopted several harsh and restrictive measures aimed at punishing Massachusetts, but particularly Boston. On March 31, 1774, King George the Third signed the Boston Port Bill, intended to severely reprimand rebellious Boston. The port was closed to all seagoing traffic until damages for the destroyed tea were paid in full. The Massachusetts Provincial Charter of 1691, which residents viewed as a sacred guarantee of their liberties, was revoked. Additional regiments of regulars were dispatched to Boston and Major General Thomas Gage replaced Thomas Hutchinson as governor. Gage moved the seat of government from Boston to Salem and the customs office from Boston to Plymouth. The Governor's Council was replaced with a non-elective Mandamus Council, town meetings were prohibited without the consent of the governor and jury trials were abolished.

To the citizens of Massachusetts, it was clear that the British government had thrown down the gauntlet. Passage of these "Intolerable Acts," as they became known, was seen as the most blatant of the attempts by England to provoke a war with her American colonies. Throughout the colonies, committees of correspondence toiled to spread this message and increase opposition to Parliament. Towns adopted covenants asserting their opposition to the British attempt to crush their rights, while Middlesex and Essex counties ordered its courts to refrain from conducting business. On September 26, 1774, Lexington voted to form committees whose responsibilities were "to bring two pieces of cannon from Watertown and mount them, to provide a pair of drums for the use of the military company in town . . . [and] to have the militia and alarm list meet for a view of their arms."[106] On October 5, 1774, Lexington's Deacon Stone was in Salem

---

[106] Declarations and Resolves, Town of Lexington, September 26, 1774.

along with his fellow representatives to the General Court. There, when General Gage acted to arbitrarily adjourn the General Court, the representatives voted to make the Massachusetts Provincial Congress the governing body of the colony, in order "to promote the true interests of his Majesty, in the peace, welfare and prosperity of the Province."[107]

Any hope of avoiding a civil war now seemed dashed. In Boston, Hugh Earl Percy correctly surmised the state of affairs in Massachusetts on the eve of the American Revolution. "Things here are now drawing to a crisis every day. The people here openly oppose the New Acts. They have taken up arms in almost every part of this Province, & have drove in the Gov't & most of the Council . . . A few days ago, they mustered about 7,000 men at Worcester . . . In short, this country is now in an open state of rebellion."[108]

---

[107] Massachusetts Provincial Congress, Wednesday, October 5, 1774.
[108] Letter from Percy to the Duke of Northumberland, September 12, 1774.

~4~

A Good Fire Arm: The Lexington Militia

When war with England appeared inevitable, the
Massachusetts Provincial Congress looked to the colony's
militia to serve as its military arm. The origins of the
Massachusetts militia can be traced back to the reign of
Edward I, when Parliament enacted legislation decreeing that
every freeman between the age of fifteen and sixty was to be
available to preserve the peace within his own county or shire.[109]
In the towns where the freemen were located, they were
organized into military units known, by the virtue of their
periodic training, as "trained bands". However, when
Parliament, under the rule of Charles II, revised membership
requirements, established payment protocols and appointed
officers, trained bands became known as militias. By the 17th
century, militias had become one of the cornerstones of
English society. Thus, when Plimouth and Massachusetts Bay
colonies were founded, the establishment of the militia
followed naturally. In both colonies, every man over sixteen

---

[109] Edward M. Harris, *Andover in the American Revolution*, (Marceline,
Missouri: Walsworth Publishing Company, 1976), 37.

automatically became a member. Musters were frequent and mandatory, and punishments were doled out for being absent or not properly equipped. The governor maintained the sole authority to activate the militia in the time of crisis. Each time a new town sprung up, a militia company was formed. As the town expanded, additional companies often were created. When counties were formed, the various town militias within the borders of each county were organized into regiments. The governor held the sole authority to activate the militia in the time of crisis. However, with the elimination of the French threat as a result of the French and Indian War, the need for a militia decreased significantly. After 1763, companies and regiments of Massachusetts militia rarely assembled to drill and as a result, were of little military value. By the eve of the Boston Tea Party, a militia muster was not viewed as a military gathering, but rather as a sort of town holiday offering an opportunity for families and friends to get together.

As relations with England worsened, the Massachusetts Provincial Congress moved to wrest control of the militia away from the group of elderly loyalist officers who commanded it. To achieve this, the Provincial Congress ordered the militias to "meet forthwith and elect officers to command their respective companies; and that the officers so chosen assemble as soon as may be . . . and proceed to elect field officers."[110] Congress also recognized the need to revitalize and further strengthen the colony's militia system as quickly as possible.

On October 26, 1774, the Congress voted to create a Committee of Safety, charged with the responsibility to "carefully and diligently . . . inspect and observe all and every such person or persons as shall at any time attempt or enterprise the destruction, invasion, detriment or annoyance of this Province . . . [The Committee] shall have the power . . . to

---

[110] Massachusetts Provincial Congress, Wednesday, October 26, 1774.

alarm, muster, and cause to be assembled with the utmost expedition, and completely armed, accoutered . . . march to the place of rendezvous, such and so many of the militia of this Province, as they shall judge necessary for the ends aforsaid."[111] To support the logistical needs of the Committee of Safety, a sister committee was created to gather "such provisions as shall be necessary for [the militia's] reception and support, until they shall be discharged by order of the Committee of Safety."[112] In the same stroke, the congressional delegates set in motion the process of creating minuteman companies.

In the decades following the establishment of the initial English settlements in Massachusetts, the number of hostile encounters had continually increased between the colonists and the French and Native Americans who opposed further English expansion west and north into New England.[113] To counter the ever-present threat of French and Native American attacks, Massachusetts created rapid response militia units that evolved over time into the minutemen. During King Phillips's War (1675-1676), Massachusetts ordered one hundred men from each county regiment "to be ready at an hour's warning and . . . not fail to be at the [appointed] rendezvous."[114] With the outbreak of King George's War in 1745, militia commanders were again required to appoint a fraction of their men "to be [ready] at a minutes warning to march [to the] enemy."[115] When the French and Indian War started, Massachusetts continued to make use of the rapid-response concept. Militia companies were required to single out particular men "to be completely

---

[111] *Ibid.*
[112] *Ibid.*
[113] In response to this threat, Massachusetts Bay Colony decentralized its tactical control of the militia and on September 7, 1643, allowed "in cases of danger and assault, to raise the whole force of the country . . . and to draw them together to [a place] necessary [for the] defense of the country." John R. Galvin, *The Minute Men The First Fight: Myths and Realities of the American Revolution*, (Washington D.C.: Brassey's Inc., 1989), 10.
[114] *Ibid*, 25.
[115] *Ibid*, 30.

furnished with arms and ammunition . . . and hold themselves in readiness to march at a minute's warning to such part of the [frontier] or elsewhere as service required."[116] Thus, in 1774, it was natural for the Provincial Congress to continue this model, requiring

> [The] field officers, so elected, forthwith [shall] endeavor to enlist one quarter, at the least, of the number of the respective companies, and form them into companies of fifty privates . . . who shall equip and hold themselves in readiness, on the shortest notice from the said Committee of Safety, to march to the place of rendezvous . . . said companies into battalions, to consist of nine companies each.[117]

Acting upon these instructions, the recently elected militia officers loyal to the Provincial Congress traveled throughout their respective counties recruiting minutemen. Andover's Samuel Johnson, colonel of the 4th Essex Regiment of Militia, appeared before each of his companies to recruit and organize companies of minutemen.[118] On February 2, 1775, he spoke to the two companies of Andover's North Parish militia. At the conclusion of his lecture, fifty men rushed forward, "more than a third part of whom [were] heads of families and men of substance and probity" to enlist.[119] That same day, in the town's South parish, forty-five men immediately enrolled, being "rather . . . animated . . . by the late disagreeable news contained in the King's speech."[120]

Most towns had little or no problem finding men who were willing to fill the ranks of minuteman companies. However, to ensure enlistments, many towns established an annual salary for those who joined the ranks of minuteman

---

[116] *Ibid*, 41.
[117] *Ibid*.
[118] Report of the Committee Appointed by the Town of Andover, November 14, 1774.
[119] *Ibid*.
[120] *Ibid*.

companies. Concord passed a resolution stating that
minutemen would receive "reasonable wages" for service.
Worcester established a pay scale structure in the event
hostilities erupted. Andover resolved that its minutemen
would receive

> [From the] 25th of October to . . . the 30th day of
> March . . .. eight pence for each half day they shall be
> exercised in the art of military . . . and from 30th day
> of March to the 30th Day of September . . . one shilling
> for each half day they shall be exercised . . . and in the
> case each soldier shall be called to active service, thirty
> six shillings per month.[121]

Over the years, efforts had been made to establish the
minimum requirements of arms and accoutrements when
fielding with the militia. Early in the colony's history,
Massachusetts required "Every listed souldier ... shall be
always provided with a well fixt firelock musket, of musket
or bastard musket bore, the barrel not less then three foot and a
half long, or other good firearms to the satisfaction of the
commission officers of the company, a snapsack, a coller with
twelve bandeleers or cartouch-box, one pound of good
powder, twenty bullets fit for his gun, and twelve flints, a
good sword or cutlace, a worm and priming wire fit for his
gun."[122] Another early militia law required a militiaman to

---

121 Report of the Committee Appointed by the Town of Andover,
November 14, 1774. In the months after the Provincial Congress'
minuteman order, many towns went to great lengths to see that its
minutemen and militia were properly armed, equipped and trained.
Andover, Lincoln and Acton equipped each of its minute companies with
bayonets, muskets and cartridge boxes. Galvin, 65; In Dudley, a military
staff was created to "assist in settling and establishing of the minnut men."
Harris, 69; In Haverhill, the town paid a publisher in England to print a
copy of the Norfolk Exercise. When the copy arrived, the town hired a Mr.
George Marsden for thirty dollars to "train the militia in the art of
military." G.W. Chase, *History of Haverhill*, (Haverhill, Massachusetts:
self-published, 1861), 375.
122 Massachusetts Militia Laws, Nov. 22, 1693.

keep "his firelock in good repair, four pounds of lead in bullets, fitted to the bore of his piece, four flints, a cutlass or tomahawk, a good belt round his body, a canvas knapsack to hold a bushel, with a good matumpline, fitting easy across the breast and shoulders, good clothing, etc."[123]

Despite popular modern misconceptions, Massachusetts colonists were not a poorly equipped army. Instead it appears most towns took appropriate steps to ensure its soldiers were well equipped for war.[124] Thus, as tensions increased between the army in Boston and Massachusetts colonists, the surrounding towns instinctively began to issue resolves setting forth guidelines for its militia and minute companies. On December 26, 1774, Roxbury ordered "Militia minutemen [to] hold themselves in readiness at a minutes warning, compleat in arms and ammunition; that is to say a good and sufficient firelock, bayonet, thirty rounds of powder and ball, pouch and knapsack."[125] The following month, Braintree required each soldier furnish himself with "a good

---

[123] Source undated and unknown, but original shown to Henry Cooke by Peter Oakley in 1995.

[124] After the Battles of Lexington and Concord, Massachusetts continued to set down basic militia guidelines. In 1776, under the guidance of Colonel Timothy Pickering of Salem, Massachusetts attempted to again establish a uniform equipment system by requiring each soldier to own "a firelock, bayonet, waist belt, a cartridge box, cartridges, and a knapsack." Timothy Pickering, *An Easy Plan of Discipline for a Militia*, (Salem, 1775) p. 1-4. In 1778, the Third Bristol County Militia Regiment wanted their men to have the following at muster: "a good firearm with steel or iron ramrod, and spring to retain the same, a worm, priming wire and brush, and a bayonet fitted to his gun, a tomahawk or hatchet, a pouch containing a cartridge box that will hold fifteen rounds of cartridges at least, a hundred of buckshot, a jack knife, and tow for wadding, six flints, one pound of powder, forty leaden balls fitted to his gun, a knapsack and blanket, a canteen or wooden bottle sufficient to hold one quart." *Continental Journal and Weekly Adviser*, January 22, 1778. Another early company document mentions "a powderhorn, a bullet pouch to contain 40 leaden balls, a knapsack, a canteen, a firearm of good worth, a haversack, a belt, a good pair of overalls." *Boston Gazette*, May 26, 1777.

[125] Town of Roxbury Resolves, December 26, 1774.

fire lock, bayonett, cartouch box, one pound of powder, twenty-four balls to fitt their guns, twelve flints and a knapsack."[126] In Bridgewater, it was expected "each soldier to provide himself with a good fire arm, a steel or iron ram rod and a spring for same, a worm, a priming wire and brush, a bayonet fitted to his gun, a scabbard and belt thereof, a cutting sword or tomahawk or hatchet, a . . .cartridge box holding fifteen rounds . . . at least, a hundred buckshot, six flints, one pound of powder, forty leaden balls fitted to the gun, a knapsack and blanket, [and] a canteen or wooden bottle to hold one quart [of water]."[127]

Militia and minutemen obtained their weapons from a variety of sources. These sources included imported muskets sold by local merchants[128]; muskets and equipment captured from enemy troops (most notably the French and Spanish)[129];

---

[126] Town of Braintree Resolves, January 23, 1775.

[127] Journal of Arthur Harris of the Bridgewater Coy of Militia.

[128] "To be sold by John Pim of Boston, Gunsmith, at the Sign of the Cross Guns, in Anne-Street near the Draw Bridge, at very Reasonable rates, sundry choice of Arms lately arrived from London, viz. Handy Muskets, Buccaneer-Guns, Fowling Pieces, Hunting Guns, Carbines, several sorts of Pistols, Brass and Iron, fashionable swords, &c." (*Boston Newsletter*, July 11, 1720); "Newly imported, and sold by Samuel Miller, Gunsmith, at the Sign of the Cross Guns near the Draw-Bridge, Boston: Neat Fire Arms of all sorts, Pistols, Swords, Hangars, Cutlasses, Flasks for Horsemen, Firelocks, &c." (*Boston Gazette*, May 11, 1742)

[129] "We killed and took about the same number of the enemy. The lieuttenant of the British company and myself, were foremost, and we advanced on and found their sleeping-place, and while running it up, the Lieutenant was shot through the vitals and he died soon thereafter. Thus I was all alone, the remainder of our party not having gained the summit; the enemy retreated, and i followed them to the other end of the hill. In my route on the hill, I picked up a good French gun and brought it home with me." (*The Life of Captain David Perry, A Soldier of the French and Revolutionary Wars*). As militiamen from the village of Lynn marched off to war on April 19, 1775, an observer noted "[one man with] a long fowling piece, without a bayonet, a horn of powder, and a seal-skin pouch, filled with bullets and buckshot. . . Here an old soldier carried a heavy Queen's arm with which he had done service at the conquest of Canada twenty years previous, while by his side walked a stripling boy with a

locally produced weapons; stands of arms issued by the British government to Massachusetts provincial and militia soldiers during the French and Indian War; and finally, the *rare* procurement of a musket from a willing British soldier stationed in Boston.

Historically, during the French wars of the 17th and 18th Centuries Massachusetts Bay Colony encouraged its provincial soldiers to provide their own arms, rather than rely upon the government. For example, Governor Pownall declared in the Boston Gazette that "as most people in North America have arms of their own, which from their being accustomed to and being so much lighter than the Tower Arms, must be more agreeable and proper for them, General Amherst, as an encouragement for their coming provided with good muskets, engages to pay every one they shall so bring that may be spoiled or lost in actual service at the rate of twenty-five shillings sterling."[130] Jonathan Barnard of Waltham, Massachusetts petitioned the Massachusetts colony to be reimbursed for the loss of a firearm by his son who was killed "in a battle near Lake George".[131]

Thus, it was not uncommon to observe within the same militia company, 20 gauge fowlers, 12 gauge fowlers, 1742 King's Pattern musket (often and erroneously referred to as the 1st Model Brown Bess),[132] Dutch muskets,[133] Spanish

---

Spanish fusee not half its weight or calibre, which his grandfather may have taken at the Havana, while not a few had old French pieces, that dated back to the reduction of Louisbourg." (*History of Lynn*, p. 338)

[130] *Boston Gazette*, March 26, 1759.

[131] *Journals of the House of Representatives of Massachusetts*, Volume XXXIV, part 2, page 253.

[132] The 1742 King's Pattern was the successor to the 1730 pattern and represented the majority of muskets shipped from England to Massachusetts during the French and Indian War. The 1742 musket's overall length was 61 11/16 inches, its barrel length was 45 1/2 inches and its caliber was .77. This firelock featured a double bridled firelock, a wood ramrod, a brass nose band to slow wear on the fore end of the stock and a redesigned oval trigger lock. All furniture was brass.

muskets, American muskets with parts obtained from several sources and French muskets within the same militia company. In Lexington, militiaman Benjamin Locke's musket was of French origin;[134] Captain John Parker's musket was a combination of English, American and French parts[135] and several other militiamen fielded with fowling pieces. As militiamen from the village of Lynn marched off to war on April 19, 1775, an observer noted

> [one man with] a long fowling piece, without a bayonet, a horn of powder, and a seal-skin pouch, filled with bullets and buckshot. . . Here an old soldier carried a heavy Queen's arm with which he had done service at the conquest of Canada twenty years previous, while by his side walked a stripling boy with a Spanish fusee not half its weight or calibre, which his grandfather may have taken at the Havana, while not a few had old French pieces, that dated back to the reduction of Louisbourg.[136]

The militiamen and minutemen of Massachusetts carried their bullets and powder in various ways. Frequently, a militiaman would obtain a horn from a slaughtered cow, boil out the inner material, fill it with gunpowder and insert wooden stoppers on both ends to prevent the powder from falling out. They might personalize it by engraving it with

---

[133] Dutch muskets were generally 61 3/8 inches in length; its barrel was 45 7/8 inches and had a caliber of .78. Its furniture was composed of iron or brass, the ramrods were made of wood and the lock plate was rounded (as opposed to flat). It is the author's estimate that at least 4585 British and Dutch muskets remained in the hands of the Massachusetts provincials by 1759.

[134] Benjamin Locke's musket is currently in the possession of the Lexington Historical Society.

[135] John Parker's musket is currently on display in the senate chambers of the Massachusetts Statehouse.

[136] Alonzo Lewis and James P. Newhall, *History of Lynn, Essex County, Massachusetts 1629 - 1864*, (Salem, Massachusetts: Higginson Book Company), 338.

maps, slogans or pictures. A leather or linen strap was then
attached to the horn, and slung over the left shoulder. A shot
pouch usually accompanied the powder horn. These leather
bags usually held bullets, buckshot, flints and other necessary
supplies. Like the horn, the hunting bag was suspended over
the left shoulder.

A large percentage of the American forces also used
cartridge boxes. A list of men and accouterments from a
militia regiment in Bristol County included "Firearms - 446,
Ramrods - 129, Springs - 9, Worms - 160, Priming wires -
193, . . .Cartridge box and powder - 274."[137] In short, almost
half of the regiment's 678 soldiers were using cartridge boxes.
The most common type of cartridge box constructed on the
eve of the American Revolution consisted of a soft leather
pouch "D" design with a wooden block to hold nineteen
rounds of ammunition.[138] The box lacked side flaps and
would not have kept powder dry during inclement weather.
Many towns, including Concord, Lincoln and Acton, paid its
saddlers to make cartridge boxes for its minute and militia
companies.[139]

Bayonets were scarce in Massachusetts, and the
colony's militiamen were not as well equipped as their British
counterparts. The origins of the bayonet can be traced back to
17th century France. The first recorded military use of this
weapon by the French army was in 1642. Twenty years later,
the British army also adopted bayonets.[140] The early version
was known as the "plug bayonet": a dagger having a tapered
handle for insertion into the muzzle of a soldier's musket.[141]

---

[137] "List of Men & accouterments of Each man [illegible words] Regiment
in Bristol County [Massachusetts]" from private collection. Dated 1776.
[138] An example of such a box, with modifications made during the Siege
of Boston, is on display at Minute Man National Historical Park in
Concord, Massachusetts.
[139] For an example, see Concord Massachusetts, Town Records.
[140] George C. Neumann, Swords and Blades of the American Revolution,
(Rebel Publishing Company, Texas 1991) p. 22.
[141] Ibid.

However, the plug bayonet had its limitations. Soldiers could not fire their muskets when the bayonet was inserted in the muzzle; the plug bayonet often jammed and it was easily lost during close combat. By 1720, both England and France adopted the socket bayonet. The socket bayonet, which slipped *over* the barrel of a musket, remained in use throughout the American Revolution.

The bayonet was an offensive tool with the dual purpose of serving as a weapon during close quarter combat and, at the same time, instilling "shock and awe" in the enemy. Many 18th century European battles were decided by close combat involving edged weapons. More importantly, on more than one occasion during the Revolution, the mere sight of British or German soldiers fixing bayonets often instilled fear in undisciplined opponents and inspired the American army to flee from the field.

However, Massachusetts militiamen were very reluctant to adopt this important weapon. In his work *Swords and Blades of the American Revolution*, the late George Neuman correctly argued "When the . . . bayonet . . . gained acceptance throughout Europe in the late 1600s the Americans apparently used it sparingly . . . [Specifications] by most colonies for their militia continued to stress swords and hatchets as the recommended side arms. Bayonets appear to have finally begun to receive official endorsement during the 1740s – but even then only as an elective alternate to the sword or hatchet."[142] This perception continued through the early years of the American Revolution. An April 1775 return to the Provincial Congress indicated that only 10,108 bayonets existed for 21,549 muskets.[143] The following year, an inspection of a Bristol County militia regiment suggests that there were only 175 bayonets available for 446 muskets.[144] As

---

[142] Ibid at 23-24.
[143] Galvin, 65.
[144] "List of Men & accouterments of Each man [illegible words] Regiment

63

late as 1777, a *Boston Gazette* advertisement encouraged militia men to acquire "a powder horn, a bullet pouch to contain 40 leaden balls, a knapsack, a canteen, a firearm of good worth, a haversack, a belt, [and] a good pair of overalls," but failed to endorse bayonets.[145]

Naturally, this begs the question why was the bayonet in short supply in 18th Century Massachusetts? It appears two factors influenced this condition, economics and governmental policy. In regard to the former, many gunsmiths actually elected not to sell bayonets to their customers. For example, John Pim of Boston advertised "To be sold by John Pim of Boston, Gunsmith, at the Sign of the Cross Guns, in Anne-Street near the Draw Bridge, at very Reasonable rates, sundry choice of Arms lately arrived from London, viz. Handy Muskets, Buccaneer-Guns, Fowling Pieces, Hunting Guns, Carbines, several sorts of Pistols, Brass and Iron, fashionable swords."[146] Twenty-two years later, Samuel Miller announced "Newly imported, and sold by Samuel Miller, Gunsmith, at the Sign of the Cross Guns near the Draw-Bridge, Boston: Neat Fire Arms of all sorts, Pistols, Swords, Hangars, Cutlasses, Flasks for Horsemen, Firelocks."[147]

Although business choices severely limited a militia man's access to a bayonet, early government policy actually discouraged the use of bayonets. Most likely, officials saw little use for the bayonet on the battlefields of North America. As early as 1693, Massachusetts Militia laws dictated that

---

in Bristol County [Massachusetts]" from private collection. Dated 1776: "Men including officers - 678, Firearms - 446, Ramrods - 129, Springs - 9, Worms - 160, Priming wires - 193, Brushes - 138, Bayonets - 175, Scabbards - 142, Belts - 181, Cutting swords & hatchets - 255, Cartridge box and powder - 274, Buckshot - 10373, Jackknives - 403, Tow for men - 258 flints for men - 2084, pounds powder - 244 1/2, Bullets - 11934, Knapsack - 365, Blankets - 386, Canteens - 295"
[145] *Boston Gazette* May 26, 1777.
[146] *Boston Newsletter*, July 11, 1720.
[147] *Boston Gazette*, May 11, 1742.

"Every listed souldier ... shall be alwayes provided with a well
fixt firelock musket, of musket or bastard musket bore, the
barrel not less then three foot and a half long, or other good
firearms to the satisfaction of the commission officers of the
company, a snapsack, a coller with twelve bandeleers or
cartouch-box, one pound of good powder, twenty bullets fit
for his gun, and twelve flints, a good sword or cutlace, a worm
and priming wire fit for his gun."[148] In 1733, it was advertised
"Every listed Soldier, and other Householder shall be always
provided with a well fixt Firelock Musket, of Musket or
Bastard-Musket bore, the Barrel not less than three Foot and
an half long, or other good Fire Arms to the satisfaction of the
Commission Officers of the Company; a Cartouch Box: one
Pound of good Powder: Twenty Bullets fit for his Gun, and
twelve Flynts; a good Sword or Cutlass; a Worm, & priming
Wire, fit for his Gun, on Penalty of six Shillings..."[149]

During the French and Indian War, not all
Massachusetts provincial soldiers were issued bayonets. In
1759 only forty-nine militia men from Lexington were issued
bayonets.[150]   Likewise, many provincial soldiers who enlisted
to fight the French were only issued a "Canteen, Wooden
bottle one hoop . . . Knapsacks...Arms and Cartridge Boxes."[151]
Even on the eve of the American Revolution, regulations still
discouraged the adoption of bayonets as a primary weapon.
Massachusetts militia men were required to fall out with "his

[148] Massachusetts Militia Laws, Nov. 22, 1693. Likewise, in New
Hampshire, the colony declared "Every soldyer Shall be well provided w'th
a well fixed gun or fuse, Sword or hatchet, Snapsack, Catouch box, horne
Charger & flints." New Hampshire Militia Laws, Oct. 7, 1692.
[149] *Boston Newsletter*, February 7, 1733.
[150] "The following names are a full and Just account of those to whom I the
Subscriber delivered Bayonets in the company under my command in
Lexington, Benjamin Reed, Captain, June 5, 1759... [49 militia men
listed]" *Massachusetts Muster Rolls*, vol. 97, p. 216.
[151] Massachusetts Historical Society, *Journal of the House of
Representatives*, vol. 35, p. 287 and 335; Acts and Resolves, Public and
Private, of the Province of the Massachusetts-Bay, p. 313; *Diary Kept at
Louisbourg, 1759-1760, by Jonathan Procter of Danvers*, p. 70.

firelock in good repair, four pounds of lead in bullets, fitted to the bore of his piece, four flints, a cutlass or tomahawk, a good belt round his body, a canvas knapsack to hold a bushel, with a good matumpline, fitting easy across the breast and shoulders, good clothing, etc."[152]

Thus, when war seemed inevitable with England, Massachusetts militia and minute man companies scrambled to adopt bayonets. On October 25, 1774, the Massachusetts Provincial Congress ordered 5,000 bayonets produced.[153] In Lexington, the residents resolved "to provide bayonets at the town's cost for one third of the training soldiers."[154] In Roxbury, minutemen were ordered to "hold themselves in readiness at a minutes warning, compleat in arms and ammunition; that is to say a good and sufficient firelock, bayonet, thirty rounds of powder and ball, pouch and knapsack."[155] In Bridgewater, Arthur Harris noted "Each soldier to provide himself with a good fire arm, a steel or iron ram rod and a spring for same, a worm, a priming wire and brush, a bayonet fitted to his gun, a scabbard and belt thereof, a cutting sword or tomahawk or hatchet, a . . . cartridge box holding fifteen rounds . . . at least, a hundred buckshot, six flints, one pound of powder, forty leaden balls fitted to the gun, a knapsack and blanket, [and] a canteen or wooden bottle to hold one quart [of water]"[156]

Even as the Regulars retreated from Concord, the desperate need for obtaining bayonets was apparent. According to Sylvanus Wood, when he encountered a straggling grenadier, "I cocked my piece and run up to him, seized his gun with my left hand. He [surrendered] his armor,

---

[152] Source undated and unknown, but original shown to Henry Cooke by Peter Oakley in 1995.
[153] Resolves of Massachusetts Provincial Congress, October 25, 1774.
[154] Declarations and Resolves, Town of Lexington, December 28, 1774.
[155] Declarations and Resolves, Town of Roxbury, December 26, 1774.
[156] Journal of Arthur Harris of the Bridgewater Coy of Militia.

one gun and bayonet, a large cutlash [cutlass] and brass fender, one box over the shoulder with twenty-two rounds, one box round the waist with eighteen rounds."[157] According to official British reports, the largest pieces of equipment lost on April 19th were bayonets. "Return of the Arms & Accoutrements of the following Corps, Lost, and Broke, on the 19th April 1775 . . .Firelocks lost: 97 . . . Bayonets lost: 143 . . . Swords lost: 4 . . . Pouches with shoulder belts lost: 43 . . . Waist belts lost: 52 . . . Slings lost: 70 . . . Cartridge Boxes lost: 10 . . . Sword scabbards lost: 4 . . . Bayonet scabbards lost: 27 . . . Match cases lost: 3."

Some towns paid its residents to make bayonets. Often this involved modifications cutting down the stock of flintlocks so a bayonet could be accepted onto the barrel of the gun. Other militiamen countered the deficiency of bayonets by using other edged weapons, such as cutlasses, hangers or hatchets.

Militia and minutemen varied little in other equipment as well. Although some carried tin canteens dating back to the French and Indian War, most carried "cheesebox" canteens that were supplied by their town coopers. Styles in knapsacks appeared to be consistent as well. Many militiamen used a single pouch, double strap knapsack constructed of heavy linen or canvas.[158] Others preferred the use of blanket rolls and tumplines, a style popular both before and after Lexington and Concord.[159]

Included within this military world of the Massachusetts militia were the men from Lexington. Despite

---

[157] Pension application of Sylvanus Wood, a Massachusetts militiaman who captured a British grenadier on April 19, 1775.

[158] Sundry Petitions to the General Court, 1775 - 1778, *Massachusetts Archives*, vols 180 -183; Henry M. Cooke IV, *Knapsacks, Snapsacks, Tumplines: Systems for Carrying Food and Clothing Used by Citizens and Soldeirs in 1775*, (Randolph, Massachusetts: unpublished and undated), 1-3.

[159] *Ibid.*

popular belief, Lexington's militia was not known in 1775 as the "Lexington Minute Men". Instead, the militia company either retained its Puritan title and was known as the "Lexington Training Band"[160] or was called "Captain John Parker's Company". Period documents from the town suggest the unit was officially known as "Training Band" and its soldiers were called "training soldiers". However, depositions from Lexington militiamen in the aftermath of the Battle of Lexington refer to their town militia not as the Lexington Training Band, but as "Captain Parker's Company". It is possible that both unit designations were used interchangeably.

Lexington's militia company consisted of one hundred and thirty men, along with four officers, seven non-commissioned officers, one clerk, one fifer and one drummer. Six of the town's families furnished a total of twenty-nine. The oldest militiaman was sixty-three, while the youngest was a mere fourteen. Fifty-five men were over the age of thirty and only twenty-eight had seen combat during the two previous French wars.[161]

Complying with tradition, the training band elected its officers. In command on the eve of the Battle of Lexington was Captain John Parker, a forty-six year old large-framed man consumed by tuberculosis.[162] His second in command was thirty-eight year old Lieutenant William Tidd. Serving as the training band's first ensign was sixty-three year old Robert

---

[160] In November of 1774, the selectmen of the town voted to tax itself "forty pounds for the purpose of mounting cannon, ammunition, for a pair of drums for the use of the Training Band in the town and for carriage and harness for burying the dead." Lexington Town Records, November 10 - December 27, 1774, Lexington Town Hall.

[161] It is this author's contention that despite popular belief, Captain John Parker was not among the twenty-eight veterans of the French and Indian War. His name does not appear on any regimental muster roll and he was a landowner at the outset of the war (and thus had no reason to leave Lexington.). See Anderson, 26 -39.

[162] Tourtellot, 49.

Munroe. Unlike his two superior officers, he was a veteran of
both the Siege of Louisbourg in 1745 and the French and
Indian War. The second ensign was Joseph Simmonds and the
clerk was Daniel Harrington. William Munroe, the young
proprietor of Munroe's Tavern, served as the company's
orderly sergeant, while Francis Brown and Ebenezer White
also held the rank of sergeant. Four corporals were also
elected by the company: Joel Viles, the town's hog reeve;
Samuel Sanderson; John Munroe, the youngest son of Ensign
Munroe and Ebenezer Parker, the youngest of all the officers.[163]

   In the fall and winter of 1774, Lexington had begun to
take steps to establish a minuteman company, as evidenced by
the vote on December 28, 1774 "to provide bayonets at the
town's cost for one third of the training soldiers."[164]
However, such a company was never officially formed. It is
possible that part of the blame rested with its regimental
commander. Lexington's militia company belonged to the 1st
Middlesex Regiment of Foote, a militia regiment composed of
companies from Waltham, Lexington, Menotomy,
Charlestown, Medford, Malden, Cambridge, Newton,
Watertown and Weston. The 1st Middlesex's commander,
Thomas Gardner of Watertown, never issued orders to the
companies of his regiment to organize minuteman units.
Thus, on April 19, 1775, the Lexington Training Band only
had militiamen within its ranks.

   On the eve of the American Revolution, Lexington was
actively preparing for war. In November of 1774, the
selectmen of the town voted to tax itself "forty pounds for the
purpose of mounting cannon, ammunition, for a pair of drums
for the use of the Training Band in the town and for carriage
and harness for burying the dead."[165] Edmund Munroe
observed that the men of Lexington pledged to "improve

---

[163] *Ibid.*
[164] Declarations and Resolves, Town of Lexington, December 28, 1774.
[165] Lexington Town Records, November 10 - December 27, 1774,
Lexington Town Hall.

ourselves in the art of military [and] . . . to meet in order for discipline."[166] As late as April 18th, a squad of Lexington militia men met with Lieutenant Tidd either at his house or on the Common to drill.[167]

It is unknown what military drill Lexington's militia utilized. It is possible that the training band used the Norfolk Exercise. Developed in England in 1757, the Norfolk Exercise, or "A Plan of Discipline, Composed for the Use of the Militia of the County of Norfolk", had been adopted by many New England militia companies by 1768 and was declared the official drill of the colony in the early 1770's. The drill called for fifty consecutive movements, each with a separate order, in the priming, loading and firing of a musket. Platoons formed three ranks, one behind the other, the front rank kneeling and the other two standing. In tight formation, each rank, platoon or company would fire a massive volley, reload and then fire again. The procedure would continue until the soldiers were ordered to cease-fire.

However, the Norfolk Exercise was not the only military drill available to Massachusetts militia. On October 29, 1774, the Massachusetts Provincial Congress ordered that "it be recommended to the inhabitants of this Province that in order to their perfecting themselves in the Military Art, they proceed in the method ordered by his Majesty in the year 1764, it being, in the opinion of this Congress, best calculated for appearance and defence."[168] Known as the 1764 Crown Manual of Arms, this was the drill used by the British troops stationed in Boston in 1775. The object of the drill was to compensate for the limitations of the inaccurate muskets of the time.[169] Men were concentrated in close ranks, shoulder to

---

[166] Charles Hudson, History of the Town of Lexington, *Genealogies*, Vol. I, (Boston: Houghton Mifflin Company, 1913), 226.
[167] Deposition of Ebenezer Munroe, April 2, 1825.
[168] Massachusetts Provincial Congress, Saturday, October 29, 1774.
[169] Despite popular belief, 18th century British soldiers were taught to aim. According to the journal of Lieutenant Frederick Mackenzie of the 23rd

shoulder so as to present a massed array of muskets. The men were to fire in unison only upon command and then to reload as rapidly as possible.[170] The attacking force would advance until they reached a point of eighty yards away from their enemy. After firing a volley, the force would advance to fifty yards where a second and perhaps a third volley would be fired. Then, the attacking force turned to the bayonet.[171] Speed and precision honed by hours of practice, combined with iron discipline, were the requisites necessary for men to continue loading and firing even while their comrades fell around them.[172]

The major challenge faced by Lexington's militia was the scarcity of gunpowder. It was expensive and the town had a very limited supply. However, the militia did possess several advantages that partially offset their lack of ammunition. Every member of the militia was familiar with the surrounding countryside and knew the locations that offered military advantages. Over half of the militia resided close enough to the village common to assemble on short notice. Lexington also had several residents who owned fast horses and could serve as scouts and alarm riders. However, the men of Lexington would need every one of these advantages should they be forced to confront the Regulars if

---

Welsh Fusiliers, "15th Jany [1775]. The Regiments are frequently practiced at firing with ball at marks. Six rounds pr man at each time is usually allotted for this practice. As our Regiment is quartered on a Wharf which projects into part of the harbour, and there is a very considerable range without any obstruction, we have fixed figures of men as large as life, made of thin boards, on small stages, which are anchored at a proper distance from the end of the Wharf, at which the men fire. Objects afloat, which move up and down with the tide, are frequently pointed out for them to fire at, and Premiums are sometimes given for the best Shots, by which means some of our men have become excellent marksmen."

[170] John O. Newell, *Battle Road 1998*, (Weston, Massachusetts: unpublished, 1998) 1.

[171] Anthony Darling, *Red Coat and Brown Bess*, (Alexandria Bay, New York: Museum Restoration Service, 1993), 11.

[172] *Ibid.*

and when His Majesty's forces decided to march out from
Boston.

~5~

Enemies of This People:

The Hours Before The Battle of Lexington

       When Parliament passed the Boston Port Bill, in an attempt to break the Massachusetts colonists of their resistance to crown policy, it also authorized General Gage to undertake any military measures necessary to help bring the colony under control. Gage quickly responded by ordering naval warships to the New Hampshire coast, Cape Ann and to Boston's south and north shores. He dispatched scouts to Concord and Worcester with instructions to map the roads and topography, sample the political moods of the countryside and discover what they could about the provincial supply depots located in both towns.

On September 1, 1774, Gage ordered a picked force of his regulars to seize the largest supply of gunpowder in the colony, 250 half barrels, stored in a magazine on Quarry Hill, then part of the town of Medford, but now Powder House Square, Somerville. The raid started at 4:30 in the morning and was successfully completed by first light. Five months later, on February 26, 1775, 240 men of the 64th Regiment of Foot landed in Marblehead and marched to Salem with orders to seize twenty cannons located within the seaside town. However, unlike the September 1st raid of the previous year, the colonists of Essex County were aware of the object of the mission from the outset. Militia and minute companies from the surrounding communities quickly mobilized. After a tense standoff with the Salem militia, the regulars were forced to return to Boston empty-handed.

In late winter and early spring of 1775, Gage received a series of dispatches from London ordering him to not only arrest the leaders of Massachusetts's opposition party, but to launch a major strike against the apparently growing provincial stockpiles of weapons and munitions. As he contemplated these orders, Gage considered a variety of military options, including a long-range strike against the large store of weapons located in the shire town of Worcester, forty miles west of Boston. Realizing that this was much too risky a venture, the general decided instead to seize the military supplies reportedly stored at Concord, a march half the distance of that to Worcester.

It appears Gage's primary desire when drafting his orders was the recovery of four brass cannons. On the eve of the American Revolution, brass cannons were considered "weapons of mass destruction". They were light, easily maneuverable and deadly. In September 1774, four brass cannons were stolen while under guard by Boston residents and smuggled out of the town. In February, 1775, the Massachusetts Provincial Congress reported the guns were located in Concord. The next month, Gage's informants

confirmed the pieces were "Conceal'd at Mr. B, (lately chose
or appointed Minute Colo.) Suppos'd to be deposited in his
cellar."[173]

Gage's plan called for approximately seven hundred
men composed of the elite grenadiers and light infantry from
several regiments and a company of marines, to march from
Boston to Concord under cover of darkness on April 18, 1775.[174]
This "strike force," under the command of Lieutenant Colonel
Francis Smith of the 10th Regiment of Foot, was ordered "
[You are to proceed] with the utmost expedition and secrecy
to Concord where you will seize and destroy all the artillery,
ammunition, provisions, tents, small arms and all military
stores whatever. But you will take care that the soldiers do not
plunder the inhabitants, or hurt private property."[175] Gage
instructed Smith to dispose of provincial supplies by
destroying the trunions of the cannons, burning the tents,
dumping powder and shot into local ponds and eradicating
food "in the best way you can devise."[176] To counter the
problem of colonial alarm riders spreading word of the
expedition, the general informed Smith that "a small party on
horseback is ordered out to stop all advice of your march
getting to Concord before you."[177]

Unfortunately for Gage his carefully prepared plan did
not carry through as he expected. As the operation date
neared, the general unintentionally sent a series of warning
signs to the Boston populace that a raid into the countryside
was about to occur. As Lieutenant MacKenzie correctly
noted, "[the] people of the Country are extremely jealous of
these movements and some of them constantly attend,
apparently to observe if there is any particular object in view,

---

[173] http://www.nps.gov/mima/planyourvisit/the-hancock.htm
[174] Fischer, 313.
[175] Orders from General Thomas Gage to Lieutenant-Colonel Francis
Smith, 10th Regiment of Foot, April 18, 1775.
[176] *Ibid.*
[177] *Ibid.*

and to convey intelligence if necessary."[178] Throughout
March and April of 1775, British regiments were ordered to
repair camp equipment and gear.[179] On April 5th, the Royal
Navy, at Gage's request, began to prepare for a movement of
troops by water. Two days later, transport boats were
launched and repaired in full view of civilian onlookers. On
April 10th, the 38th and 52nd Regiments "marched out . . . as far
as Watertown and did not return to Boston 'till 5 oClock in the
Afternoon."[180] Finally, on April 15th, Gage ordered the
"Grenadier and Light Infantry companies . . .to be off duty 'till
further orders, as they will be ordered out to learn the
Grenadier Exercise, and some new evolutions for the Light
Infantry."[181] From observing this conduct, Massachusetts
correctly anticipated that a major operation was about to be set
in motion. On April 18, 1775, that anticipation became
reality.

As Solomon Brown, an eighteen-year-old Lexington
boy, was returning home from the market in Boston on the
evening on April 18, 1775, he had no idea he was about to
stumble across the advance guard of a British force bound for
Concord. About six o'clock that evening as he neared
Lexington, he spotted nine British officers riding slowly along
the country road before him. The evening was not very cold
yet Brown noted that each of the officers was wearing a heavy
wool blue overcoat under which he could see the shape of

---

[178] Diary of Lieutenant Frederick MacKenzie, March 28, 1775.
[179] Fischer at 86; "As the tents belonging to our regiment have all been
repaired, we pitched them on Fort Hill this day, by way of airing them, and
seeing that everything was in proper order." Diary of Lieutenant Frederick
MacKenzie, April 11, 1775.
[180] Diary of Lieutenant Frederick MacKenzie, April 10, 1775. Three days
earlier, MacKenzie noted "As Regiments are often ordered to take marches
. . . from this order, and several other circumstances, it is supposed the
General has some object in view, and means to familiarize the people of
the Country with the appearance of Troops among them for a longer than
usual, without creating an alarm." Diary of Frederick MacKenzie, April 7,
1775.
[181] Diary of Lieutenant Frederick MacKenzie, April 15, 1775.

their pistols. Taken aback, Brown passed the officers and galloped on to Lexington. He rode directly to Munroe's Tavern where he informed Sergeant Munroe of what he had observed.

Sergeant Munroe quickly dispatched a detail to guard the provincial leaders John Hancock and Samuel Adams, who had taken up temporary residence a short distance up the Bedford Road from the tavern in the home of Reverend Clarke. According to Munroe, "these men were placed . . . around the house of Mr. Clarke for the night and I remained with them."[182] At eight o'clock, the town received two messages from Elbridge Gerry, a member of the Provincial Committee of Safety and Supplies. According to Jonas Clarke,

> We received two messages, the first verbal, the other, by express, in writing from the Committee of Safety, who were then sitting in the westerly part of Cambridge, directed to the Honorable John Hancock, Esq., who, with the Honorable Samuel Adams, Esq., was then providentially with us, informing that eight or nine officers of the king's troops were seen just before night passing the road towards Lexington in a musing, contemplative posture; and it was suspected they were out upon some evil design. Both these gentlemen had been frequently, and even publicly, threatened by the enemies of this people, both in England and America, with the vengeance of the British administration. And as Mr. Hancock, in particular, had been more than once personally insulted by some officers of the troops in Boston, it was not without some just grounds supposed that under coverage of the darkness, sudden arrest, if no assassination might be attempted by these instruments of tyranny.[183]

[182] Deposition of Sergeant William Munroe, April 25, 1822
[183] "A Brief Narrative of the Principle Transactions of That Day" by Jonas

By nine o'clock that evening, after the party of British officers had been observed riding through Lexington, thirty members of the training band had assembled outside Buckman's Tavern. Among those present were Solomon Brown, Jonathan Loring and Elijah Sanderson. An older member of the alarm list, encouraged to locate the nine officers and ascertain their objective, approached the three. The young men agreed to set out on their horses. Sanderson and Loring were charged with the task of observing the officer's movements, while Brown would ride ahead to Concord to alert the town. Half an hour later, the three were captured in Lincoln. "We were, about ten of the clock, suddenly surprized by nine persons, whom we took to be Regular Officers, who rode up to us, mounted and armed, each having a pistol in his hand, and after putting pistols to our breast, and seizing the Bridles of our horses, they swore, that if we stirred another step, we should be all dead men, upon which we surrendered our selves."[184]

About two hours later, alarm rider Paul Revere rode into Lexington. He galloped past Munroe's Tavern, across the bridge at Vine Brook and on to Buckman's Tavern. After a brief conversation with the men there, he rode the few hundred yards up the Bedford Road to the Clarke parsonage. As he dismounted, Revere encountered Sergeant Munroe and his armed guard. Munroe, not recognizing the rider, called for Revere to identify himself and ordered him not to make so much noise as people inside the house were trying to sleep.

The agitated Revere shouted "Noise! You'll have enough noise before long! The regulars are coming out!" Storming past the sergeant, he began banging on the front door

Clarke, A.M., Pastor of the Church in Lexington, Massachusetts State, April 19, 1776.
[184] Depositions of Elijah Sanderson, Solomon Brown and Jonathan Loring, April 25, 1775.

of the parsonage. Hancock immediately lifted the sash of his bedroom window to see what was happening. Recognizing Revere, he exclaimed, "Come in Revere! We're not afraid of you!"[185]

Revere hastily entered the home and informed Adams and Hancock that the Regulars had left Boston and were probably at that moment marching towards Lexington. Shortly afterwards, a second alarm rider, William Dawes, arrived to confirm Revere's report. Reverend Clark wrote later, "[between] the hours of twelve and one on the morning of the 19th of April, we received intelligence, by express, from the intelligence service, the Honorable Joseph Warren, Esq. at Boston, that a large body of the king's troops, supposed to be a brigade of about twelve or fifteen hundred, were embarked in boats from Boston and gone over to land on Lake Marispoint, so-called, in Cambridge."[186]

Revere, Dawes, Adams, Hancock and Clarke left the parsonage and walked down Bedford Road to Buckman's Tavern to speak with the officers of the training band. According to Clarke, the conversation centered on the purpose of the British mission[187] and after some debate, it was concluded that the goal of capturing Adams and Hancock was at best secondary. Instead, "it was shrewdly suspected that they were ordered to seize and destroy the stores of arms belonging to the colony, then deposited at Concord, in consequence of General Gage's unjustifiable seizure of the provincial magazine of powder at Medford, and other colony stores, in several other places."[188] With no word from Brown, Loring or Sanderson, it was deemed necessary to try to again carry the warning to Concord. Revere and Dawes immediately set out, and as they galloped away from the town at about one thirty in the morning, Lexington's alarm bell

---

[185] Fischer, 110.
[186] Clarke, "A Brief Narrative . . ."
[187] *Ibid.*
[188] *Ibid.*

began to toll out its warning.

As Clarke recalled, "upon this timely intelligence, the militia of this town were alarmed, and ordered to meet on the usual place of parade."[189] As they gathered, Captain Parker addressed his men so as to "consult what might be done for our own and the people's safety; and also, to be ready for whatever service Providence might call us out to upon this alarming occasion, in case--just in case--overt acts of violence or open hostilities should be committed by this mercenary band of armed and blood-thirsty oppressors."[190] After some discussion, it was decided to confirm the accuracy of Revere's message by sending scouts eastward to locate and observe the movements of the British regulars. "Two persons were sent, express, to Cambridge, if possible to gain intelligence of the motions of the troops and what route they took. The militia met, according to order, and waited the return of the messengers that they might order their measures as occasion should require."[191]

The two scouts traveled along separate routes and were gone for several hours. One of the two returned between three and four o'clock in the morning and reported that there was "no appearance of the troops on the roads to Cambridge and Charlestown and that the movements of the army were but a feint to alarm the people."[192] Believing Revere was mistaken, Parker dismissed his men "but with orders to be within call of the drum, waiting the return of the other messenger who was expected in about an hour, or sooner, if any discovery should be made of the motions of the troops."[193] Some of the militia went home, but many walked across the village common to Buckman's Tavern. Before entering, they discharged their muskets into the air.

---

[189] *Ibid.*
[190] *Ibid.*
[191] *Ibid.*
[192] *Ibid.*
[193] *Ibid.*

Meanwhile, Revere and Dawes were experiencing some difficulty of their own. According to Revere,

> We set off for Concord, and were overtaken by a young gentleman named Prescot, who belonged to Concord, and was going home. When we had got about half way from Lexington to Concord, the other two stopped at a house to awake the men, I kept along. When I had got about 200 yards ahead of them, I saw two officers as before. I called to my company to come up, saying here was two of them, (for I had told them what Mr. Devens told me, and of my being stopped). In an instant I saw four of them, who rode up to me with their pistols in their bands, said "G---d d---n you, stop. If you go an inch further, you are a dead man." Immediately Mr. Prescot came up. We attempted to get through them, but they kept before us, and swore if we did not turn in to that pasture, they would blow our brains out, (they had placed themselves opposite to a pair of bars, and had taken the bars down). They forced us in. When we had got in, Mr. Prescot said "Put on!" He took to the left, I to the right towards a wood at the bottom of the pasture, intending, when I gained that, to jump my horse and run afoot. Just as I reached it, out started six officers, seized my bridle, put their pistols to my breast, ordered me to dismount, which I did.[194]

Captured by the same officers who had caught Brown, Sanderson and Loring earlier, Revere was subjected to a series of interrogations. As the evening wore on, the questioning intensified into open threats of violence. "One of them (whom I since learned was Major Mitchel of the 5th Reg.) clapped his pistol to my head, and said he was going to ask me some questions, and if I did not tell the truth, he would blow my brains out. I told him I esteemed myself a man of truth, that

---

[194] Draft Deposition of Paul Revere, April 24, 1775

he had stopped me on the highway, and made me a prisoner, I knew not by what right; I would tell him the truth; I was not afraid. He then asked me the same questions that the other did, and many more, but was more particular; I gave him much the same answers. "[195]

At the same time, Revere also fed the officers a good deal of misinformation as well. He began by telling them "I knew what they were after; that I had alarmed the country all the way up, that their boats were caught aground, and I should have 500 men there soon."[196] He warned them that the countryside was alarmed and if they remained in the vicinity of Lexington, they would be in extreme danger.

The officers were shaken by Revere's information. They were almost sixteen miles from Boston and according to their captive, in the midst of hostile territory. The men quickly remounted, ordered their captives to do the same and warned their prisoners "we are now going towards your friends, and if you attempt to run, or we are insulted, we will blow your brains out."[197] The nine officers formed a circle, placed their four prisoners in the center of it and hurried back towards Lexington. When they were half-a-mile from the village common, a gunshot rang out. Major Mitchell, the party leader, demanded clarification, and when Revere informed him that it was to alarm the country, Mitchell "ordered the four prisoners to dismount, they did, then one of the officers dismounted and cut the bridles and saddles off the horses, and drove them away . . . I asked the Major to dismiss me, he said he would carry me, let the consequence be what it will. He then ordered us to march."[198] As the party neared the

---

[195] *Ibid.* Nor were the three Lexington captives immune from questioning either. "They detained us until Two O'clock the next morning, in which time they searched and greatly abused us; having first enquired about the magazine at Concord, whether any guards were posted there, and whether the bridges were up." Brown, Loring and Sanderson Deposition.
[196] Revere Deposition.
[197] *Ibid.*

village common, they began to hear the alarm bell clanging rapidly. A few moments later, the riders were startled by musket fire from the direction of Buckman's Tavern.[199] Loring, following Revere's lead, turned to his captors and exclaimed "The bells a ringing! The towns alarmed and you're all dead men!"[200]

Recognizing the gravity of the situation, Mitchell quickly consulted with his fellow officers. Afterwards, the officers approached the three Lexington men and then released them.[201] As for Revere, Mitchell

> asked me how far it was to Cambridge, and many more questions, which I answered. He then asked the sergeant, if his horse was tired, he said yes; he ordered him to take my horse. I dismounted, and the sergeant mounted my horse; they cut the bridle and saddle of the sergeant's horse, and rode off down the road.[202]

Revere and the others left the road and "waded through the swamp, through mud and water, hoping to arrive at the meeting house before [the officers] could pass, to give information to [the militia]."[203] But Major Mitchell and his fellow officers fled too quickly to be captured, riding through Lexington at break-neck speed, stopping only briefly before the meetinghouse, and then galloping off towards Cambridge. When Revere and the others arrived at the tavern, Sanderson observed that the "citizens were coming and going; some went down to find whether the British were coming; some came back and said there was no truth in it."[204] Young Sanderson quickly refreshed himself with a quick drink, slumped into a

---

[198] *Ibid.*
[199] The volley was most likely fired by a party of militiamen who were clearing their muskets before entering the tavern.
[200] Deposition of Elijah Sanderson, December 17, 1824.
[201] Brown, Loring and Sanderson Deposition.
[202] Revere Deposition.
[203] Sanderson Deposition.
[204] *Ibid.*

chair by the fire and fell asleep.

Revere, however, went directly to the Clarke residence to ensure that Hancock and Adams had left Lexington. Upon discovering that the two had not, he quickly ushered them into a heavy coach and dispatched them to Woburn.[205] As the two rode away, Hancock's clerk, John Lowell, approached Revere. He hurriedly informed the alarm rider that his employer had forgotten a large trunk containing documents crucial to the colonial cause in the upper chamber of Buckman's Tavern. Recognizing the potential intelligence windfall if the documents fell into Gage's hands, the two raced down Bedford Road and returned to the tavern.

As Revere and Lowell entered, Thaddeus Bowman, the second scout sent out earlier in the morning came galloping up Boston Road. Reigning in his horse at Buckman's, he shouted to Captain Parker that the Regulars were less than a half hour away. Parker immediately summonsed the training band's sixteen-year-old-drummer, William Diamond. Diamond, who as a child worked in a tavern in Cambridge before being taken in as a servant by Lexington's Abijah Child, had been taught to play the drum by a British soldier in Boston. That morning, as signal guns were fired and the alarm bell rang, the boy drummer in answer to Parker's command began to beat the call to arms.[206] Militiamen converged on the village common from all directions.

Revere and Lowell ran up the tavern stairs to the

---

[205] Although I do not contest that Samuel Adams uttered the historic words of "What a glorious day for America!" I do challenge the location of where it was uttered. After reading the deposition of Paul Revere, it is this author's opinion that Hancock and Adams were at least three miles away from the Lexington Common when the battle started. It is more likely that the statement was uttered in Woburn when news of the battle reached them. If anything, the location of where the words were said was changed for both political and propaganda purposes.

[206] Source: Research conducted by Steve Cole of the Lexington Minute Men, 2001.

second floor to recover Hancock's trunk. The two men, according to Revere, "made haste, and had to pass through our militia, who were on a green behind the Meeting House, to the number as I supposed, about 50 or 60."[207] Once clear of the militia, the two men made a desperate dash for a line of woods adjacent to the common and out of harms way.

As they fled into the woods, Sergeant Munroe was assembling the men into ranks near the meetinghouse. Captain Parker then ordered his company to the right about face and marched them a further seventy-five yards away from the meetinghouse and from the road to Concord. When the company had covered the distance, he ordered his men to halt and execute a second right about face, which left them somewhat to the rear of the common, and facing the meetinghouse. Parker then turned to his men and said "[let] the Troops pass by, and don't molest them, without they begin first."[208]

As the company stood waiting, more militiamen continued to file onto the common. The precise number that actually made it onto the field by the time of the battle is in dispute. Some give the figure of seventy-seven as commemorated on the battle-site monument, but not all those so enumerated actually were standing in formation on the common. The number in ranks may have been as low as some fifty odd.[209] As the growing thunder of drums and marching feet began to echo across the common, the militiamen began to stir and look hesitantly about. The regulars were out, and the Captain John Parker's Company was directly in their path.

---

[207] Revere Deposition.
[208] *Ibid.*
[209] Fischer, 189 and 400.

~6~

Without They Begin First: The Battle of Lexington

The regular soldiers and officers marching towards the Lexington militia were in an understandably foul mood. The expedition, under the command of Lieutenant-Colonel Smith of the army and Major John Pitcairn of the Royal Marines, consisted of over seven hundred men. The force was composed of one company of marines, and the grenadier and light infantry companies of eleven different regiments.[210] The troops had begun crossing the Charles River by boat at ten o'clock at night and completed their landing at Phips Farm in Cambridge shortly after midnight. For the next two hours, the entire expedition stood in the freezing marshes until rations that they did not need arrived and were handed out.

When the expedition finally got under way at two o'clock in the morning, Colonel Smith soon realized that the entire countryside seemed to know of its existence. As Smith reported days later, "notwithstanding we marched with the utmost expedition and secrecy, we found the country had

---

[210] The eleven regiments were: The 4th, 5th, 10th, 18th, 23rd, 38th, 43rd, 47th, 52nd and the Royal Marines.

intelligence or strong suspicion of our coming, and fired many signal guns, and rung alarm bells repeatedly."[211] Realizing that the expedition was running behind schedule and that the success of the mission was in jeopardy, Smith halted the column upon reaching Menotomy. There, he gave his men a short rest and summonsed Pitcairn. He ordered the Major to take the six companies of light infantry and "march with all expedition to seize the two bridges on different roads beyond Concord."[212] Pitcairn set off immediately, pushing his detachment hard, and sent forward an advance guard consisting of Lieutenant Jesse Adair of the Royal Marines, loyalist guide Daniel Murray, several other officers and eight light infantrymen.

As Pitcairn's force pushed forward, the advance guard captured two alarm riders, Asahel Porter and Josiah Richardson of Woburn. As the two riders were taken into custody, signal guns and alarm bells began to sound. Hearing the alarms, Smith +ordered an officer to return to Boston to request reinforcements. At the front of Pitcairn's column the sound of many galloping horses was heard, and into the ranks of the advance guard rode Major Mitchell's party which had earlier captured Revere and three Lexington riders. As Lieutenant William Sutherland of the 38th Regiment of Foot remembered, "[we] were joined by Major Mitchell . . . and several other gentlemen who told us the whole Country was alarmed and had Galloped for their lives, or words to that purpose."[213]

Yet, Pitcairn was determined to press ahead to Concord. As the expedition marched forward, a third alarm rider, Simon Winship of Lexington, was captured. However, unlike his two predecessors, he refused to dismount and had to be dragged off his horse at gunpoint.[214] The column

[211] Report of Lieutenant-Colonel Smith to General Gage, April 22, 1775.
[212] *Ibid.*
[213] Letter from Lt. William Sutherland to Major Kemble, April 27, 1775.
[214] Deposition of Simon Winship, April 25, 1775.

encountered other individuals on the road that morning both on horse and on foot. Each of them, when questioned by the officers, emphasized that a large body of militia was gathered in Lexington and would resist the regulars if they continued their march to Concord.[215]

As the column crossed into Lexington, Lieutenant Sutherland physically collided with Benjamin Wellington, a thirty-one-year-old Lexington resident who had his musket and bayonet in hand. "I . . . mett one of them in the teeth whom I obliged to give up his firelock and bayonet, which I believe he would not have done so easily but for Mr. Adair's coming up."[216] Wellington was forced to surrender his musket and then ordered to go home. Instead, he hurried back to the village common and rearmed himself with another musket from the town's supply of weapons stored in the meetinghouse.

As the column closed in on Lexington's common, a British sergeant reported that a party of colonial horsemen rode out from the village and shouted, "[you] had better turn back, for you shall not enter the town!" One of the mounted men then "presented a musquet and attempted to shoot them, but the piece flashed in the pan."[217] According to Lieutenant Sutherland, another individual fired at him from the vicinity of Buckman's Tavern.[218] He reported this to Pitcairn who then galloped to the front of the column, halted the men and ordered them to load their muskets.[219] "On this, I gave

---

[215] *Ibid.*

[216] *Ibid.*

[217] Letter from Major Pitcairn to General Gage, April 26, 1775.

[218] "A fellow from the corner of the road on the right hand Cock'd his piece at me, burnt priming. . . we did not return [fire]"

[219] "Simon Winship of Lexington, declared that being upon the road about four o'clock, two miles and an half on this side of the meeting house, he was stopped by the Regulars, and commanded by some of the officers to dismount or he was a dead man; that he obliged to march with the said Troops until he came within about half a quarter of a mile of the said meeting house, when an officer commanded the Troops to halt, and then to

directions to the troops to move forward, but on no account to Fire, or even attempt it without Orders."[220]

William Sutherland noted "shots fired to the right and left of us, but as we heard no whissing of balls, I [concluded] they were to Alarm the body that was there of our approach."[221] Off in the distance, militiamen could be seen hurrying into line. "The road before you go into Lexington is level for about 1000 yards . . . when we came up to the main body which appeared to me to Exceed 400 in and about the village who were drawn up in a plain opposite the church."[222]

Captain Parker's men waited nervously for the arrival of the British regulars. As the troops approached, many began to realize the danger they were in. One was bold enough to tell Parker "There are so few of us! It is folly to stand here!"[223] The militia captain, ignoring the outcry, turned to his company and stated "Let the troops pass by, and don't molest them, without they begin first."[224]

Pitcairn now faced a military quandary. If he chose to ignore the militia company drawn up on the village common, he would be leaving an armed opponent to his rear. If he halted, he could exacerbate an already tense situation.[225]

The light infantry officers in the lead company of the column, the 4th Regiment of Foot, resolved Pitcairn's dilemma

---

prime and load." *An account of the commencement of Hostilities between Great Britain and America, in the Province of the Massachusetts-Bay. By the Reverend Mr. William Gordon of Roxbury, in a Letter to a Gentlemen in England, dated May 17, 1775;* Fischer, 187.

[220] Pitcairn to Gage.

[221] Sutherland to Kemble.

[222] *Ibid.*

[223] Deposition of Sylvanus Wood, June 17, 1826.

[224] Revere Deposition. According to legend, Captain Parker stated, "The first man who offers to run shall be shot down! Stand your ground! Don't fire unless fired upon! But if they mean to have a war, let it begin here!" William Munroe Deposition; See Fischer 400, Fn 21.

[225] Fischer, 189.

by directing their men towards the Lexington militia. The next regiment, the 10th Regiment of Foot, quickly followed. The two lead companies raced towards the increasingly nervous militia. Suddenly, they deployed into a line of battle and began to shout "Huzzah!"[226] Pitcairn, realizing the situation was getting out of hand, "instantly called to the soldiers not to fire, but rather to surround and disarm the militiamen."[227] Many of the excited troops may never have heard this order as they continued to shout their "huzzahs!" Perhaps some of the officers also did not hear his order. Lieutenant Edward Gould of the 4th Foot later testified that he could not hear above the noise his men were making.[228]

Pitcairn and other officers rode towards Captain Parker and his men. According to Sutherland, several officers began to shout, "throw down your arms and you shall come by no harm, or words to that effect."[229] Private James Marr of the 4th Foot believed Pitcairn exclaimed, "Stop you rebels!"[230] However, many of the Lexington militiamen later asserted that the officers shouted "Lay down your arms, Damn you, why don't you lay down your arms?"[231] Militiaman John Robbins, who was in the front rank of the training band as the regulars approached, recalled the officers chastised the militia by stating, "Throw down your arms ye Villians, ye Rebels!"[232]

---

[226] Depositions of Thomas Rice Willard, April 23, 1775. The battle cry "huzzah" is actually pronounced "hu zay". As the lights from the 4th and 10th Regiments surged forward, Pitcairn, from his vantage point further back, recognized what had occurred. He rode ahead and redirected three of the companies that had not marched onto the common back onto Concord Road. However, at the same time, an unidentified officer steered the light company of the 5th Regiment of Foot onto Bedford Road.

[227] Pitcairn to Gage.

[228] Deposition of Lieutenant Edward Thronton Gould of His Majesty's Own Regiment of Foot, April 25, 1775.

[229] Sutherland to Kemble.

[230] Gordon, "An account of the commencement of Hostilities . . ."

[231] Willard Deposition.

[232] Deposition of John Robins, April 24, 1775.

Spectator Thomas Fessenden heard an officer order "Disperse
you rebels, immediately."[233] Jonas Clarke, believed he heard
an officer demand "Ye villains! Ye rebels! Disperse, damn
you! Disperse!"[234]

Recognizing the situation was becoming more and
more dangerous; Parker turned to his men and issued new
orders. "I immediately ordered our militia to disperse, and not
to fire."[235] Most of the men obeyed his command and began
to file off the common. Some, however, either did not hear
Parker's order or chose to ignore it. As a result, several
Lexington men held their ground as the light infantry surged
forward.

Suddenly, a single shot rang out. Revere, who was still
in the woods with Lowell, said later he could not determine
the source of the shot. Lieutenant Edward Gould also stated
he could not determine the source of the shot, as his men were
making too much noise. Many of the British officers believed
a provincial fired the mysterious shot. Major Pitcairn reported
that "some of the rebels who had jumped over the wall, fired
four or five shott at the Soldiers, which wounded a Man of the
Tenth, and my horse was wounded in two places, from some
quarter or other, and at the same time, several shott were fired
from a meeting house on our left."[236] According to Lieutenant
Sutherland, "instantly, some of the Villains who got over the
hedge fired at us which our men for the first time returned."[237]
Even Lieutenant Colonel Smith asserted "[our] troops
advanced towards them, without any intention of injuring
them, further than to inquire the reason of their being thus
assembled, and if not satisfactory, to have secured their arms;
but they in confusion went off, principally to the left, only one
of them fired before he went off, and three or four more

---

[233] Deposition of Thomas Fessenden, April 23, 1775.
[234] Clarke, "A Brief Narrative . . .".
[235] Deposition of John Parker, April 25, 1775.
[236] Pitcairn to Gage.
[237] Sutherland to Kemble.

jumped over a wall and fired from behind it among the
soldiers; on which the troops returned it."[238]

Months later, as he lay dying from wounds sustained at
Bunker Hill, Major Pitcairn again spoke of the Battle of
Lexington. According to Ezra Stiles, Pictairn asserted he was
"riding up to them, he ordered them to disperse; which they
did not do instantly, he turned about and ordered his troops to
draw out so as to surround and disarm them. As he turned, he
saw a gun in a peasant's hand, from behind a wall, flash in the
pan without going off; and instantly, or very soon, two or three
guns went off . . . [the] guns he did not see; but believing they
could not come from his own people, and that thus, they began
the attack."[239]

From the provincial point of view, the first shot was
from the King's army. Simon Winship described an officer on
horseback "flourishing his sword, and with a loud voice,
giving the word fire, fire, which was instantly followed by a
discharge of arms from the said regular troops."[240] Nathan
Munroe contradicted William Sutherland when he stated he
stumbled over a wall into John Buckman's land, about six rods
from the British, and then turned and fired at the regulars only
after they had fired at him first.[241] Jonas Clarke insisted one
of the mounted officers with the expedition fired the first shot.
"The second of these officers, about this time, fired a pistol
towards the militia as they were dispersing. The foremost,
who was within a few yards of our men, brandishing his
sword, and then pointing towards them, with a loud voice said
to the troops: 'Fire! By God, fire!'--which was instantly
followed by discharge of arms from the said troops, succeeded
by a very heavy and close fire upon our dispersing party, so
long as any of them were within reach."[242] John Robbins

---

[238] Smith to Gage.
[239] Diary of Ezra Stiles, August 19, 1775.
[240] Winship Deposition.
[241] Deposition of Nathan Munroe, December 22, 1824.
[242] Clarke, "A Brief Narrative . . ."

agreed with him, stating, "the foremost of the three officers order'd their men, saying fire, by God, fire! At which moment we received a very heavy and close fire from them."[243] Even John Bateman, a British soldier with the 52nd Regiment of Foot, declared he "was in the Party marching to Concord, that I heard the word of command given to the troops to fire, and some of the troops did fire."[244]

Although the source of the shot will never be known, what happened next is. The light infantry began to fire either with or without orders. "Upon hearing the report of a pistol or gun, then the Regulars huzzaed and fired, first two more guns, then the advanced guard and so the whole body."[245]

At first, the militiamen thought the regulars were firing blanks. Yet, when Elijah Sanderson saw a light infantryman fire at a man behind a stone wall, he observed "the wall smoke with bullets hitting it. I realized they were firing balls."[246] Ebenezer and John Munroe also believed the troops were firing only powder until Ebenezer Munroe was wounded in the arm. Angered by his injury, the militia man returned fire, screaming, "I'll give them the guts of my gun!"

With the volley, the spectators gathered along the edges of the common broke and ran. Timothy Smith, who was watching the events unfold, recalled that he "immediately ran, and a volley was discharged at me, which put me in imminent danger of losing my life."[247] Thomas Fessenden later testified, "I ran off as fast as I could."[248] Benjamin Tidd and Joseph

---

[243] Deposition of John Robins, April 24, 1775.
[244] Deposition of John Bateman, April 23, 1775. Samuel Lee, a private in the 18th Foot asserted Pitcairn "fired his pistol, drew his sword and ordered them to fire." Gordon, "An account of the commencement of Hostilities . . ."
[245] Gordon, "An account of the commencement of Hostilities . . ." For a detailed description of this volley, *see* Fisher, 195.
[246] Fischer, 195.
[247] Deposition of Timothy Smith, April 25, 1775.
[248] Fessenden Deposition.

Abbot of Lincoln lost control of their horses, as did Lieutenant
Sutherland whose horse bolted, carrying him through the ranks
of the fleeing militia and several hundred yards down Bedford
Road.[249]

The regulars continued to fire, "made a huzza" and
rushed furiously towards the retiring militia.[250]   As the light
infantry surged forward, Ebenezer Munroe remembered Jonas
Parker

> standing . . .with his balls and flints in his hat, on the
> ground between his feet, and heard him declare he
> would never run. He was shot down at the second fire
> . . . I saw him struggling on the ground, attempting to
> load his gun . . .As he lay on the ground, they [ran] him
> through with the bayonet.[251]

John and Ebenezer Munroe also returned fire.
According to John Munroe, he retreated ten rods, fired and
then reloaded, ramming two lead balls down the barrel of his
musket. The force of the charge took off a foot of his
musket's barrel. Ebenezer Munroe believed "there was no
chance for escape and that I might as well fire my gun as stand
still and do nothing."[252] In an interview with the Reverend
Gordon, James Brown stated "being got over the wall, and
seeing the soldiers fire pretty freely, he fired upon them, and
others did the same."[253] According to Lieutenant Tidd, he
retreated "up the north road and was pursued about thirty rods
by an officer on horseback . . . I found I could not escape him
unless I left the road. Therefore I sprang over a pair of bars,
made a stand and discharged my gun at him; upon which he

---

[249] Sutherland to Kemble.
[250]   Deposition of Captain John Parker, April 25, 1775; Deposition of
William Draper, April 25, 1775. "The balls flew so thick, I thought there
was no chance for escape." Deposition of Ebenezer Munroe, April 2,
1825.
[251] Deposition of Ebenezer Munroe, April 2, 1825.
[252] *Ibid.*
[253] Gordon, "An account of the commencement of Hostilities . . ."

immediately returned to the main body."[254]

Solomon Brown ran across Bedford Road, hopped over a stone wall and fired at the regulars. When they returned fire, the young man ran into Buckman Tavern through the back door. Once inside, he sprinted over to the front door, kicked it open and fired two more shots. Believing that Brown's actions would lead to the tavern being burned to the ground, Buckman physically ejected Brown from the establishment; forcing him to seek cover in the woods.[255]

Yet very few militiamen returned fire. Nathaniel Mulliken stated, "not a gun was fired, by any person in our company, on the regulars."[256] A year later, the Reverend Clarke strongly asserted, "far from firing first upon the King's troops; upon most careful inquiry it appears that very few of our people fired at all and even they did not fire till, after being fired upon by the troops, they were wounded themselves."[257] Several militiamen later testified "we attended the beat of our Drum, and were formed on the Parade; we were faced towards the Regulars then marching up to us, and some of our Company were comeing to the parade with their backs towards the Troops, and Others on the parade, began to Disperse when the Regulars fired on the Company, before a Gun was fired by any of our company on them."[258] The British sustained only three light injuries. Yet, the toll was very heavy for the Lexington Training Band. Eight men were killed and ten more were wounded in the brief encounter.

---

[254] Deposition of William Tidd, December 29, 1824.

[255] "As I left the field, I saw a person firing at the British troops from Buckman's back door . . . I was afterward told . . . that the same person, after firing from the back door, went to the front door of Buckman's house and fired there." Deposition of William Munore, March 7, 1825.

[256] Deposition of Nathaniel Mulliken, April 25, 1775.

[257] Clarke, "A Brief Narrative . . ."

[258] Depositions of Nathanael Parkhurst, Jonas Parker, John Munroe, jun. John Winship, Solomon Pierce, John Muzzy, Abner Meeds, John Bridge, jun. Ebenezer Bowman, William Munroe the 3d, Micah Hager, Samuel Saunderson, Samuel Hastings, and James Brown, April 25, 1775.

John Brown and Samuel Hadley were both shot in the back as they ran from the common. Jonathan Harrington was mortally wounded only a few yards from his home. Tragically, his wife and children watched as he desperately crawled towards them. He died in his wife's arms on the doorstep of his home. Woburn's Asahel Porter, who was taken prisoner earlier in the morning, was killed as he tried to flee from his captors. Caleb Harrington was killed as he exited the meetinghouse when the skirmish started. Joseph Comee was wounded in the arm as he also tried to escape the building. Remaining inside the meetinghouse, Joshua Simmonds, retreated to the upper loft where the town's supply of gunpowder was stored and thrust his loaded weapon into a barrel of powder. If the regulars attempted to storm the building, he was determined to destroy it.[259]

As the slaughter continued, Isaac Muzzey was killed and nine more militiamen were wounded, including the African-American slave Price Estabrook. In the space of five minutes, perhaps nearly one-third of the members of the Lexington Training Band who had mustered on the common had become casualties.

When Lieutenant Colonel Smith arrived on the scene, the bodies of dead and wounded militiamen littered the field, his troops were firing in every direction and some were even then preparing to storm the meetinghouse and nearby homes. Major Pitcairn was desperately attempting to regain control, swinging his sword downwards "with all earnestness, as a signal to forbear or cease fire."[260] Smith realized that order must be restored, and he began to search for a drummer to sound the recall. He approached Lieutenant Sutherland, asked him "do you know where a drum is, which I found, who immediately beat to Arms . . . the men ceased firing"[261] and sullenly returned to ranks.

---

[259] Fischer, 198.
[260] Stiles, August 19, 1775.
[261] Sutherland to Kemble.

Smith gathered his officers around him. Lieutenant Sutherland continued, "Col. Smith and Major Pitcairn regretted in my hearing the too great warmth of the soldiers in not attending to their officers and in keeping their ranks and in recommending a more steady conduct to them for the future."[262] At its conclusion of the meeting, the officers and regulars resumed the march to Concord.

As the soldiers left the onslaught behind them, the spectators emerged from hiding and made their way onto the common. Many were overcome with emotion and grief at the sight of husbands, sons, brothers, cousins and neighbors lying dead or wounded on the field. As they began to tend to the wounded, over two hundred men from Woburn's militia and minuteman companies arrived in Lexington. Disturbed at what they saw, the men halted and assisted the Lexington residents in treating the wounded and carrying the dead into the meetinghouse. Afterwards, the Woburn men reassembled and resumed their march toward Concord.[263]

Suddenly, at least five British regulars who had fallen behind the main column appeared along the Boston road. The soldiers were immediately set upon and forced to surrender. They were stripped of their muskets and equipment and marched to the common. Later in the morning, the soldiers were transferred under guard to James Reed's residence in Woburn.[264] The captured muskets and equipment were re-

---

[262] *Ibid.*
[263] According to Major Loammi Baldwin of Woburn, "We mustered as fast as possible. The Town turned out extra-ordinary, and proceeded toward Lexington . . . I rode along a little before the main body, and when I was nigh Jacob Reed's I heard a great firing; proceeded on, soon heard that the Regulars had fired upon Lexington people and killed a large number of them. We proceeded on as fast as possible and came to Lexington and saw about eight or ten dead and numbers wounded."
[264] Deposition of James Reed, January 19, 1825. According to Reed, the prisoners were transferred from Woburn to Billerica. When Billerica residents objected to the presence of British soldiers in their town, the regulars were moved to Chelmsford.

distributed by Ebenezer Munroe to other Lexington
militiamen.

At ten o'clock in the morning, the Reverend Clarke led
a brief memorial service for those killed earlier. The
minister's daughter, Elizabeth, described the original burial of
the eight men killed at the Battle of Lexington. "Father sent
Jonas down to Grandfather Cook's to see who was killed and
what their condition was and, in the afternoon, Father, Mother
with me and the baby went to the Meeting House. There was
the eight men that was killed, seven of them my Father's
parishioners, one from Woburn, all in Boxes made of four
large boards nailed up and, after Pa had prayed, they were put
into two horse carts and took into the grave yard where some
of the neighbors had made a large trench, as near the woods as
possible and there we followed the bodies of those first slain,
Father, Mother, I and the baby, there I stood and there I saw
them let down into the ground, it was a little rainy but we
waited to see them covered up with clods and then for fear the
British should find them, my Father thought some of the men
had best cut some pine or oak bows and spread them on their
place of burial so that it looked like a heap of brush."[265]

Afterwards, Captain Parker assembled his men on the
village common. According to local folklore, the company
marched westward as fifer Jonathan Harrington played *The
White Cockade*. An old Jacobite tune, the song describes a
young man's enlistment and the woman he left behind:

> It was a summer's morning as I went o'er the moss
> I had no thoughts of listing 'til some soldiers did me
> cross
> They kindly did invite me to a flowing bowl in town
> They advanced me, they advanced me, they advanced
> me some money, ten guineas and a crown

---

[265] Elizabeth Clarke to Lucy Allen, April 20, 1835. Elizabeth was twelve
years old at the Battle of Lexington.

Oh yes my love has listed, he wears a white cockade
He is a handsome young man, likewise a roving blade
He is a handsome young man, he's gone to serve the
king
And my very, and my very, and my very heart is
aching all for the love of him

Oh yes my love is handsome and comely for to see
And by a sad misfortune, a soldier now is he
I hope the man that 'listed him may never happy be
And I wish that, and I wish that, and I wish that the
Hollanders would sink him in the sea

Oh may he never prosper and may he never thrive
Nor anything he turns his hand as long as he's alive
May the very ground he walks upon, the grass refuse to
grow
Since he's been, since he's been, since he's been the
only cause of my sorrow, grief and woe

Then he took out his handkerchief to wipe her flowing
eyes
Leave off your lamentations, likewise your mournful
cries

Leave off your lamentations, for I must roam the plain
We'll be married, we'll be married, we'll be married in
London when I return again

Oh yes my love is listed and I for him will rove
I'll carve his name on every tree that lies in yonder
grove
The huntsmen he will follow, the hounds they will all
cry
To remind me, to remind me, to remind me of my
ploughboy until the day I die[266]

---

[266] http://www.cam.anglia.ac.uk/~operag/music/text/lyric082.html

Well aware that the British regulars would have to pass
through Lexington on the return, women and children quickly
packed their belongings and fled into the woods along the
Bedford-Lexington line. According to Elijah Sanderson, as
the men marched off to war, the women and children had
"been so scattered and dispersed that most of them were out of
the way when [Percy] arrived". Sadly, many of those who
lived along the Concord and Boston Roads would return to
homes destroyed or plundered by the retreating soldiers. [267]

When the Lexington Company arrived at the
Lexington-Lincoln border, Parker signaled the company to
halt. Because he had not received orders from Colonel
Gardner to march further on to Concord, Parker instructed his
men to prepare for an ambush where they were.[268]

Parker selected a position on Pine Hill, which included
a house and wood lot owned by Tabitha Nelson. However, the
position also featured a steep and abrupt drop-off to the road
below. To ascend it from the road would be difficult, and any
attempt to flank the position would be slow, challenging and
deadly. [269] The majority of the men broke ranks, scrambled
halfway up the hill and formed a staggered skirmish line. To
establish a cross fire, Parker ordered others to take up
positions across from Pine Hill.[270]

---

[267] Deposition of Elijah Sanderson, December 17, 1824. Descriptions by
Andover minute men passing through Lexington later in the afternoon
described Lexington as being devastated by fire and plunder.
[268] Decades later, Nathaniel Munroe testified that the company met the
enemy within the bounds of Lincoln, but engaged them in Lexington.
Deposition of Nathanial Munroe, December 22, 1824.
[269] Only the deposition of Nathan Munroe describes the Lexington Training
Band marching towards Concord and engaging the retreating regulars.
"About the middle of the forenoon, Captain Parker, having collected part
of his company marched them towards Concord, I being with them. We
met the regulars in the bounds of Lincoln, about noon, retreating towards
Boston. We fired on them and continued to do so until they met their
reinforcement in Lexington." Deposition of Nathan Munroe, December
22, 1824.
[270] 19th and 20th century historians disagree as to the exact location of

Absent from the company was the confusion and hesitation of the earlier encounter with the British regulars. They had been beaten and swept off their common, before their neighbors, associates and families. More than anyone else on that day, the Lexington Training Band wanted revenge.[271]

Around one o'clock in the afternoon, Parker received information that the regulars had fired on minute and militiamen from several towns at Concord's North Bridge. Under heavy fire, the soldiers were now marching back towards Lexington. Already, the sound of musket fire could be heard in the distance. After some time, minute and militia men from Woburn, Bedford, Lincoln and other towns could be seen firing and scrambling through the Lincoln fields. Suddenly, the harried regulars burst into view further down the road. They were retreating hastily and in some disarray. Attempts to return the provincial fire was made, but such acts were both fruitless and a waste of ammunition. Scores of soldiers and officers were wounded or injured and many clung to horses, carts, carriages or whatever else might help them reach Boston.

Parker let the van of the harassed expedition reach his position before ordering his men to fire. The Lexington men then unleashed a volley that swept along the first four companies, instantly killing or wounding twelve of the regulars. Lieutenant-Colonel Smith was struck in the thigh and Captain Parson of the 10th Regiment of Foot, until now the only unwounded officer in his company, was hit in the arm. Major Pitcairn, realizing that the entire column was about to

---

Parker's Revenge. For example, Coburn places the engagement in Lincoln near the Nelson and Hastings homes. French placed the Training Band further east in Lexington. Hudson believes the company was positioned well inside Lincoln. However, an archeological survey conducted in 1895 revealed evidence of combat on Pine Hill located on the North side of the Lexington-Concord road. Given Jedidiah Munroe was *killed* on Pine Hill in Lexington and Lt. Colonel Smith was wounded along the Lincoln-Lexington line, it is likely Parker's Revenge was situated near said hill.
[271] Galvin, 182.

be bogged down by Parker and his men, hastily organized a return fire. Grenadier and light companies were brought up and ordered to attack Parker's right and left flanks.

The regulars advanced slowly, faltering over the natural terrain, as Parker's men continued to fire. After some effort, the soldiers succeeded in pushing the Training Band back, first to the top of the hill and then down the east side. Once at the bottom, the company disbanded and scattered into the woods. During this action at a site now called "Parker's Revenge", two more Lexington militiamen, Jedediah Munroe and Nathan Wyman, were killed.[272]

After clearing Parker and his men from their position, Pitcairn ordered the light company of the Royal Marines up onto a small hill known only as "The Bluff". As the marines provided cover, the major quickly pushed the remainder of the column past Bull Tavern and behind the protection of the hill. Although Pitcairn was able to relieve the pressure of the provincials, the delay allowed the colonists time to take up fortified positions on neighboring Fiske Hill.

As the exhausted regulars struggled up the hill, the provincials closed in to where both sides became entangled in hand-to-hand combat. In the melee, Major Pitcairn was unhorsed and injured, six regulars and two provincials were killed and dozens on both sides wounded. At Fiske Hill, panic began to set in among the enlisted men. Many began to surrender and desert, while others broke into flight. The

---

[272] S.C. Drake, *A List of the Names of the Provincials Who Were Killed in the Late Engagement With His Majesty's Troops at Concord &c.*, May, 1775. At this point, the exact role of the Lexington Training Band is unknown. There are no records that Captain Parker regrouped his men after Parker's Revenge, that the militia was present at Concord Hill or that the men harassed Percy's relief column. However, it is probable that most of the Lexington men gathered into small groups or platoons and participated in the remainder of engagements within Lexington. Thus, it is only fair to discuss the events following Parker's Revenge; Galvin, 183-184.

panicked soldiers ignored the orders of their harassed officers and made no attempt to return fire. In full retreat, the ragged column struggled up Concord Hill, the last height before reaching Lexington center. Sensing disaster, several officers presented their bayonets, and told the men that if they broke ranks they would die. Some semblance of order was restored, but as several British officers later recounted, "the entire force was at that point on the verge of complete surrender."[273] However, upon starting down Concord Hill, and with Lexington common just coming into view, the sound of wild cheering came from the vanguard. Rushing to the front, the officers saw the ranks of Earl Percy's relief column drawn up on the hills beyond Lexington center.

Over twelve hundred strong, Earl Percy's command consisted of all the line companies of four regiments,[274] two artillery crews of the Royal Artillery and a small company of loyalists. A puff of smoke and a loud boom erupted from one of the two cannons. Seconds later, there was a crash of splintering wood as the ball tore through Lexington's meeting house, scattering the nearby militia and minutemen.[275] Colonel Smith's battered and exhausted troops hurried into the protective lines of Lord Percy's forces drawn up on the ridge near Munroe's Tavern. Once there, the soldiers of the morning's expedition collapsed, crawling under trees and

[273] Report of Ensign Henry De Berniere to General Gage.
[274] The regiments were the 4th (King's Own), the 23rd (Royal Welsh Fusiliers), the 47th and the Royal Marines.
[275] "I immediately ordered the 2 field pieces to fire at the rebels, and drew up the Brigade on a height. The shot from the cannon had the desired effect, & stopped the Rebels for a little time, who immediately dispersed." Letter from Percy to General Gage, April 20, 1775. Loammi Baldwin had spent considerable time pursuing the retreating regulars. As he took up a position between the meeting-house and Buckman's Tavern, the artillery opened fire. With the balls flying near him, Baldwin retreated back behind the meeting-house. Suddenly, a ball came through near his head. As a result, he retired to a meadow north of the house. From his position, he saw the balls in the air and strike the ground. The cost to repair the damage to the meeting house was £1, 1s.

shrubs to rest in the shade, while regimental surgeons attended to the many wounded.

After Smith's expedition arrived, both of Percy's flanks became engaged in a sniper's war. Along the left flank, provincials crawled close enough to the British lines to fire upon the officers and sergeants of the Royal Welsh Fusiliers. Lord Percy wrote later, "Nor are several of their men void of a spirit of enthusiasm, as we experienced . . . for many of them . . . advanced within 10 yds. to fire at me and other officers, tho' they were morally certain of being put to death themselves in an instant."[276] The tactic proved successful for the provincials; the regulars were forced to pull back their lines and bring up their own sharpshooters as a countermeasure. Along the right flank, the situation was worse. When the 47th Regiment failed to occupy Estabrook Hill, the provincials took advantage of the opportunity to seize the high ground and open fire on the exposed troops below. As the lead balls began to rain down, the 47th suffered an increasing number of casualties.[277]

At the center of Percy's battle line, near Munroe's Tavern, the general observed that several homes offered excellent fields of fire for rebel snipers. Percy ordered the structures burned and quickly dispatched men to perform the task. Before torching the properties, the soldiers ransacked the buildings for items of value. The regulars started with Joseph Loring's property and then moved on to the homes of Matthew Mead, Benjamin Merriam, Lydia Mulliken, Joshua

---

[276] Letter from Percy to General Harvey, April 20, 1775.

[277] According to Lieutenant Frederick Mackenzie of the Royal Welsh Fusiliers, "The ground we first formed upon was somewhat elevated and commanded a view of that before us for about a mile . . . the Village of Lexington lay between both parties . . . During this time, the rebels endeavored to gain our flanks, and crept into the covered ground on either side, and as close as they could in front, firing now and then in perfect security. We also advanced a few of our best marksmen who fired at those who shewed themselves." Diary of Lieutenant Frederick Mackenzie, April 19, 1775; Galvin, 198.

Bond and John Mason. When finished, the soldiers had caused approximately £1664 in property damage.[278]

At Munroe's Tavern, hundreds of exhausted light infantrymen and grenadiers rested on the tavern lawn. Inside the establishment, nearly every room was filled with casualties, some of whom would have to be left behind when Percy began the march back to Boston. In the taproom, rowdy soldiers drained the bar dry, demolished it and then murdered the bartender, John Raymond, by shooting him in the back as he tried to flee the tavern. The total damage done to the tavern was approximately £203, 11s, 9d.[279]

By three o'clock in the afternoon, the provincials sensed Percy would soon begin the retreat back to Boston. The individual colonial snipers pulled back and large numbers of militia and minutemen took their places on the flanks and to the front and rear of the columns. Half an hour later, Percy ordered his troops to move out. It took over thirty minutes to assemble the entire brigade on Boston Road. Percy later wrote, "[as] it began now to grow pretty late, & we had 15 miles to retire, & only 36 rounds, I ordered the grenadiers and lgt infantry to move off first, & covered them with my brigade, sending out very strong flanking parties, who were absolutely necessary, as there was not a stone wall, or house, though before in appearance evacuated, from whence the rebels did not fire upon us."[280]

As the brigade moved out, the colonists lashed out at the flanks and rear of the retiring columns. "As soon as they saw us begin to retire, they pressed very much upon our rear guard, which for that reason I relieved every now and then. In

---

[278] Alexander R. Cain, *We Stood Our Ground: Lexington in the First Year of the American Revolution*, (North Andover, Massachusetts: unpublished, 1995), Appendix E.
[279] Ibid.
[280] Letter from Brigadier General Hugh Earle Percy to General Gage, April 20, 1775.

this manner we retreated . . . under an incessant fire all round us."[281] In response, the British flanking parties set upon any house they encountered along the path retreat. Residences were fired upon, stormed, looted and then torched. Although some remained standing, the Lexington homes along Boston Road beyond Munroe Tavern were left scarred with extensive damage.

Two miles further on, the column of regulars finally left Lexington. For unknown reasons, perhaps because the Lexington Training Band still had not received orders from Colonel Gardner, Captain Parker and his men ceased pursuing the regulars at the Lexington-Menotomy line.[282] As the echoes of muskets softened, the men of Lexington slung their muskets over their shoulders, wiped the gunpowder from their faces and went home to survey the damages caused by the regulars. Most were fortunate to find their homes untouched. Some, such as Deacon Joseph Loring, found their homes burnt to the ground. Others found their homes had been broken into and looted. A few found unexpected guests inside. When Samuel Hastings and his two sons, Samuel Jr. and Isaac, returned to their home along the Lincoln-Lexington line, they found a wounded grenadier inside. The soldier was tended to for several days but eventually expired. As the Hastings family prepared to bury him behind their home, they discovered their missing silver spoons in the lining of his coat.[283]

---

[281] *Ibid.*

[282] To date, the author has yet to encounter an account from a Lexington militiaman who asserted he followed the regulars into Menotomy.

[283] Four days later, on April 23, 1775, representatives from the Massachusetts Provincial Congress arrived in Lexington and deposed members of the Lexington Training Band as to the events surrounding the Battle of Lexington.

~7~

Consumed by Fire: The Siege of Boston

In the days following the Battles of Lexington and
Concord, Dr. Joseph Fiske travelled from house to house in
Lexington, along the British retreat route, tending to the
British and American wounded.[284] Meanwhile, on April 23,
1775, representatives from the Massachusetts Provincial
Congress arrived in Lexington and deposed members of the
Lexington militia as to the events surrounding the Battle of
Lexington.[285]

In Boston, the British army found itself trapped;
surrounded by an army of Massachusetts Yankees. Yet the
Massachusetts Provincial Congress and the Committee of
Safety were confronted with a dilemma. Within a very short
period of time, the provincial army surrounding the town
began to slowly disappear. Regiments lacked any organization

---

[284] Approximately six weeks later, Dr. Fiske submitted a bill for his
services to the Massachusetts Provincial Congress.
[285] See Appendixes for the depositions from participants of the Battle of
Lexington.

and soldiers were continuously coming and going. At first, militiamen left in small groups, and then by the hundreds, as lack of provisions along with the tug of responsibilities back home weakened their senses of duty. Artemas Ward, the overall commander of the American army besieging Boston, opined that soon he would be the only one left at the siege unless something was done. To meet this problem, the Provincial Congress agreed to General Ward's requests that the men be formally enlisted for a given period of time. On April 23, 1775, the legislative body resolved to raise a "Massachusetts Grand Army of 13,600 men and appoint a Committee of Supplies to collect and distribute the necessary commodities."[286]

In undertaking this venture, Massachusetts turned to the model it had followed to attract recruits for provincial regiments during the French and Indian War. When the Massachusetts government appointed a regimental colonel to serve in the French and Indian War, he was given a packet of blank commissions for officers that he could dispense as he saw fit. Often, commissions would be contingent upon the prospective officers' success in recruiting men. To secure enlistments of private soldiers, junior officers often made arrangements with prospective non-commissioned officers, promising posts as sergeants or corporals in return for their assistance in recruiting drives.[287] The colonel was also authorized to beat his drum anywhere in the province to enlist volunteers in the coming campaign. Local militia officers were prohibited from interfering with beating orders and required to muster their companies and assist the colonel and his prospective officers with the drafting of recruits.[288]

In accordance with this process, between May 4 and

---

[286] Massachusetts Provincial Congress, April 23, 1775; Henry M. Cooke, *The Massachusetts Bounty Coat of 1775*, (Randolph, Massachusetts: unpublished and undated) 1.
[287] Anderson, 40.
[288] *Ibid*, 41.

May 8, 1775, recruiters for the army besieging Boston arrived in Lexington. However, for unexplainable reasons, the recruiters hailed not from Colonel Gardner's Regiment, which Lexington belonged to before April 19th, but from Colonel Samuel Gerrish's Regiment.[289] Over those four days, twenty men from Lexington enlisted in a company commanded by Woburn's John Wood.[290] In exchange for his enlistment, which was to expire at the end of December 1775, each man was paid £5 and promised a bounty of a coat.[291]

Designated Colonel Gerrish's 25th Regiment of the Massachusetts Grand Army, the regiment was composed of 421 men predominantly from Woburn, Wenham, Ipswich, Newbury, Manchester and Rowley and was assigned to the left wing of the besieging army. Three companies were stationed in Chelsea, two at Sewall's Point and the remaining three, including John Wood's Company, were stationed in Cambridge.

While the Lexington men of Captain Wood's company bided their time in Cambridge, other militiamen from Lexington began to stream into Cambridge. In early May, the American forces began to construct fortifications in Cambridge.[292] To support this endeavor, the Committee of

---

[289] Samuel Gerrish resided in Newbury, Massachusetts.

[290] Formerly a second lieutenant in Captain Joshua Walker's Company of Colonel David Greene's 2d Middlesex Regiment of Foot, the Woburn man was given command of Gerrish's 5th Company following Congress' push to raise 13,600 quickly. The twenty men from Lexington included Ebenezer Bowman, Daniel Smith, Joseph Robinson, Asahel Stearns, Micah Hagar, Isaac Durant, John Winship, Benjamin Fiske, William Diamond, James Brown, Benjamin Hadley, Thomas Hadley, Jr., Isaac Green, Abner Mead, Asa Robinson, David Fisk, Abraham Merriam, Amos Russell, John Peck and Ezekiel Alline. Charles Hudson, *History of the Town of Lexington*, (Boston, Massachusetts, 1913), 427.

[291] Massachusetts Provincial Congress, April 23, 1775; Henry M. Cooke, *The Massachusetts Bounty Coat of 1775*, 1.

[292] Richard Frothingham, *History of the Siege of Boston and of the Battles of Lexington, Concord and Bunkerhill*, (Boston, Massachusetts: Little, Brown and Company, 1849) 106.

Safety called upon neighboring towns, including Lexington, to
provide militiamen to assist in the erection of these defensive
works. On May 4, 1775, Colonel Thomas Gardner instructed
Captain Parker to "march one half of your Company forthwith
to Cambridge to parade before the Church meeting house, and
to pursue such orders as you Shall Receive from the General
from time to time."[293] Between May 6th and May 20th,
Lexington sent three detachments to Cambridge. The first,
commanded by Captain John Parker, arrived on May 6, 1775
and remained until May 10th.[294] The second detachment,
under the command of John Bridge Jr., left Lexington on May
11, 1775. While in Cambridge, the detachment participated in
a show of force designed to impress and deceive the British
army. In the afternoon of May 13, 1775, General Israel
Putnam assembled "all the troops at Cambridge, except those
on guard . . . [they] marched into Charlestown. They were
2200 in number, and their line of march was made to extend a
mile and a half. They went over Bunker Hill and also over
Breed's Hill . . . they then returned to Cambridge."[295] Just two
days later, on May 15th, the detachment returned home.[296]
The last detachment arrived at the siege on May 16th under
the command of Edmund Munroe and remained to take part in
the siege until May 20, 1775.[297]

Meanwhile, as the weeks passed, the Lexington men of
Wood's Company quickly learned that the regiment they
enlisted in was plagued with misfortune and mismanagement,
both of which were attributable to its colonel. Although

---

[293] Letter from Colonel Thomas Gardner to Captain John Parker, May 4,
1775.
[294] Commonwealth of Massachusetts, *Massachusetts Soldiers and Sailors
of the American Revolution*, (Boston, _). The author's information is based
upon a careful examination of the service records of those members of the
Lexington Training Band who assisted in the siege in May of 1775. From
this examination, I was able to determine that Lexington dispatched three
companies of militia to Cambridge to assist in the erection of earthworks.
[295] Frothingham at 107-108.
[296] *Massachusetts Soldiers and Sailors of the American Revolution.*
[297] *Ibid.*

Gerrish reported the regiment to be completely raised on May 19, 1775, the reality was it was only at half strength. Six of the companies forced the Committee of Safety on June 3, 1775 to investigate the regiment when it petitioned to leave and form a new unit under the command of Moses Little.[298] Following a hearing before the Committee of Safety, the companies, commanded by Captains Nathaniel Wade, Benjamin Perkins, Jacob Gerrish, Ezra Lunt and Nathaniel Warner, were permitted to depart.[299] By June 17, 1775, only six of the ten companies in the regiment had been received into the Massachusetts Grand Army.[300] Additionally, the soldiers were poorly clothed and ill equipped. Gerrish even allowed the regiment to languish without a regimental staff until two days before Bunker Hill. In truth, Samuel Gerrish's reputation for command was so poor within the American army that when a militia company from Newbury learned it was to be annexed to the regiment, its soldiers threatened to return home rather than serve under him.[301]

---

[298] Frothingham at 106. On May 26, 1775, six company captains under Gerrish petitioned the Provincial Congress to leave the regiment and form a new unit. On June 2, 1775 Colonel Gerrish was notified "A number of gentlemen have presented a petition to this Congress in behalf of themselves and the men they have enlisted, praying that Captain Moses Little and Mr. Isaac Smith may be appointed and commissioned as two of the field officers over them. Six of said petitioners are returned by you as captains, as appears by your return, and the petition has been committed to a committee, to hear the petitioners and report to the Congress, and it is therefore Ordered that the said Col. Samuel Gerrish be notified, and he is hereby notified, to attend the said committee, at the house of Mr. Learned in Watertown, the 3d day of June instant, at eight o'clock in the forenoon."

[299] The next day, Congress ordered, "Resolved, that the petition be granted, as that the petitioners be directed to apply to the committee of safety, for a recommendation to this Congress, to commission Captain Moses Little as colonel of a regiment in the Massachusetts army." Afterwards, companies under the command of Captains Sprague, Pettingill, Sherman, Rogers and Corey were transferred to Gerrish's Regiment.

[300] *Ibid* at 178. The remaining four companies were not commissioned until June 22, 1775.

[301] *Ibid.* On the eve of the Battle of Bunker Hill, the negligent conduct of Gerrish became so common, that it became the focus of severe comment

Gerrish's 25th first saw action, under its incompetent commander, on June 17, 1775. On the previous evening, American forces under the command of William Prescott moved upon Charlestown Neck. The principal aim was to tighten the encirclement of Boston by seizing Dorchester Heights to the south and Bunker Hill in Charlestown to the North.[302] In actuality, the plan was flawed from the start since the Americans did not have cannons capable of reaching Boston from Bunker Hill. In addition, the Americans bypassed Bunker Hill for Breed's Hill, only seventy-five feet high and six hundred yards from Charlestown Neck. By positioning troops there, the Americans risked being cut off by British warships that controlled both Boston harbor and the mouth of the Charles River.[303]

Throughout the night, the American soldiers worked tirelessly to build an earthen fortification overlooking Boston. In the morning, when the British discovered the works on Breed's Hill, they felt compelled to launch an attack. Following a prolonged artillery bombardment from ship and shore batteries, 2,000 grenadiers and light infantry under the command of Major General William Howe embarked from the foot of Boston Common and landed on the beaches below the American position. After some debate with his officers, Howe unwisely launched a frontal assault against the 700 New Englanders on Breeds Hill, who were sheltered within the earthen redoubt, or protected by stone walls, rail fences and other hastily constructed defenses. The regulars advanced under the protection of artillery until they were almost on top of the American position. When the British advance closed to, in some cases, a mere fifty feet of the colonial defenses, the New Englanders unleashed a series of close range volleys that

---

within several military circles on both sides of the conflict. In his letters to General Gage, Dr. Benjamin Church severely criticized the abilities of Samuel Gerrish.

[302] Bernard Bailyn, "The Decisive Day is Come: The Battle of Bunker Hill", http://www.masshist.org/bh/essay.html.

[303] *Ibid.*

swept along the British battle lines, devastating its ranks. Again and again the regulars tried to advance, and again and again the murderous volleys savaged their ranks. With some British companies experiencing 75% to 90% casualties, Howe was forced to retreat to his original assault position to attempt to rally his troops. The excited New Englanders greeted the retirement with "huzzahs" and cheers.

However, the American position was not as impregnable as it appeared. As the British army advanced on Breed's Hill, General Ward found it impossible to reinforce the position. The militiamen on Bunker Hill were more than simply reluctant to join their comrades in the front lines on Breeds Hill; the majority categorically refused to move forward, and their commanders shared their hesitancy. Most militia companies simply walked away from the fight. An alarmed General Ward correctly surmised that if the desertions continued, not only would the British win the day, but they might sweep away the colonial left flank leaving the way open to an assault on the American headquarters in Cambridge. Ward called upon every available regiment to the fight. Gerrish's Regiment, including Wood's Company, was quickly assembled in Cambridge and marched off towards Charlestown Neck.

As Ward struggled to shore up American defenses, the Committee of Safety dispatched alarm riders to the countryside. The riders quickly spread the news that the battle had commenced and that militia companies would be needed to help stem the British tide should they break through the American positions on Breeds and Bunker's Hill.[304] The "Bunker Hill Alarm", as it became known, reached Lexington sometime in the afternoon. Captain Parker ordered the Lexington Training Band to assemble and personally led sixty-four men to Cambridge to assist in the cause.[305]

---

[304] Interview with Bunker Hill National Historical Park, October 4, 2001.
[305] *Massachusetts Soldiers and Sailors of the American Revolution.*

In the meantime, Gerrish's 25th Massachusetts
Regiment had arrived at Charlestown Neck shortly after the
first assault on Breed's Hill. The battalion immediately came
under heavy fire. As Major Loammi Baldwin recalled, "[I]
went with the recruits and met men from the fort or
breastwork where there was a great number of cannon shot
struck near me, but they were not suffered to hurt me."[306]
Upon seeing the narrow roadway being raked from both sides
by British warships, Colonel Gerrish was overcome with fear.
"A tremor seiz'd [Gerrish]. He began to bellow, 'Retreat!
Retreat! Or you all be cutt off!' which so confused and scar'd
our men, that they retreated most precipitately."[307] Moments
later, Connecticut's General Israel Putnam arrived on the
scene, fresh from the fight and intent on leading
reinforcements back to the American position. He found
Gerrish prostrate on the ground, professing that he was
exhausted.[308] The general pleaded with Gerrish to lead his
troops onto the field. Finding both the colonel and the entire
regiment unresponsive, Putnam resorted to threats and
violence, cursed and threatened the men even striking some
with the flat of his sword in an attempt to drive them forward.[309]
Only Christian Febiger, the regimental adjutant, and a handful
of men who rallied around him, crossed over the neck,
climbed Bunker Hill and moved forward to take up a
defensive position on Breed's Hill.[310] In the midst of the
confusion, Thomas Doyle, a private in Captain William
Roger's Company, was killed. The remainder of the regiment
scattered and fled back towards Cambridge, where they
remained for the rest of the day. Following the American
defeat at Bunker Hill, "a complaint was lodged against

---

[306] Letter from Loammi Baldwin to his wife, June 18, 1775.
[307] An unknown Newbury man, writing on June 21, 1775, relates Gerrish's
conduct. This excerpt of the letter appears in Richard M. Ketchum,
Decisive Day, (New York, New York: Anchor Books, 1962), 165.
[308] Frothingham at 143.
[309] Ketchum at 165.
[310] Frothingham at 179. It is not known whether those who followed
Febiger onto the field included men from Lexington.

[Garish], with Ward, immediately . . . who refused to notice it, on account of the unorganized state of the army."[311] But blame did not rest with the colonel alone. Period depositions are equally critical of his entire regiment.[312] Years later, General Putnam's son would bitterly complain about Gerrish's Regiment, stating "But those that come up as recruits were evidently most terribly frightened, many of them, and did not make up with that true courage that their cause ought to have inspired them with."[313]

On June 18, 1775, as the American lines attempted to recover from the loss of the strategic Bunker Hill, the Lexington Training Band departed from Cambridge and returned home. For John Parker, it would be the last time he would participate in the siege. On September 17, 1775, he died of consumption. Shortly afterwards, Lieutenant John Bridge Jr. was elected captain of Lexington's militia company. For those who returned home with Parker on June 18th, life in the tiny dairy community would be far different from what they had experienced prior to April 19th. As the siege of Boston continued, Lexington became a supply depot for the besieging army outside of Boston, and its militiamen spent many a day guarding powder and cannons stored on the village common.

In the weeks after the Battle of Bunker Hill, the Provincial Congress turned its attention towards providing the coats that were promised to those who enlisted to serve on military expeditions. On June 29, 1775, it resolved that 13,000 coats would be provided and the total would be divided among the towns based upon their population. A committee was appointed to work out the details.[314] On July 5, 1775, Committee resolved

---

[311] *Ibid.*
[312] *Ibid.*
[313] Letter from Daniel Putnam, October 19, 1825; Frothingham at 143, FN 1.
[314] Cooke at 1.

That 13,000 coats be provided as soon as may be, and one thereof given to each non-commissioned Officer & Soldier in the Massachusetts forces agreeable to the reolves of Congress . . . Resolved, that the said 13,000 coats be proportioned immediately on all the towns and districts in this colony except the Town of Boston and Charlestown . . .which towns & districts are desired to cause them to be made of good plain cloth . . .and to be delivered to the Committee of Supplies without Buttons, at or before the first Day of [October] next and sooner if possible.[315]

In the days after the resolution, a circular letter drafted by the Provincial Congress was received by Lexington's selectmen. The letter instructed the town that

In obedience to the order of Congress, we have proportioned Thirteen Thousand Coats on all the towns and districts in this colony, excepting Boston and Charlestown, and have included you the Proportion with their resolves, and a sample as a direction to you as to the color and quality of the cloth which shall be manufactured by you and the quality of the imported cloth of which the coats shall be made: We are to assure you that the coats you supply shall be delivered to the men of your town so far as circumstances will permit.[316]

If the town fathers previously had been oblivious to the logistical shortcomings that plagued the army, they were soon made aware of the challenge that faced those attempting to supply the troops. In a postscript,

---

[315] Massachusetts Provincial Congress, July 5, 1775; Cooke at 1 - 3. The committee also provided descriptions of the proposed coat and established a fee schedule for production.

[316] Circular Letter to the Selectmen of Stoughtonham, July 6, 1775; Cooke at 2. The sample attached to the letter that served as a guide appeared to have been between fawn and tobacco brown in color. *Ibid* at 3.

the Provincial Congress pleaded with the selectmen that "a large number of shirts, stockings and summer breeches are wanted immediately for the use of the Army, you are therefore requested, as . . . the lives and health of your Countrymen, to furnish this Committee as soon as possible with a large number of said articles, not less than two shirts, two pair of stockings and two pair of summer breeches."[317]

As tailors and women in Lexington worked feverishly to make "bounty coats", the men of Wood's Company remained in Chelsea, dividing their time between observing British operations and collecting cattle for the American army.[318] The humdrum routine of the siege was shaken when General George Washington reached Cambridge late in the evening of July 2, 1775, and then formally opened his headquarters the following day.

The Commander in Chief made it quite clear from the outset that his mission was to turn the various forces assembled around Boston into a unified army.[319] He recognized that regiments from the different New England colonies arrived at Boston in 1775 in a rather piecemeal fashion and occupied positions dictated principally by the terrain and the road network. On July 22, 1775, Washington attempted to impose a more rational organizational structure by issuing orders dividing the American army into three divisions of six brigades each, and assigning the various general accordingly. [320] He also adapted the command structure to the specific geographical conditions and

---

[317] Circular Letter to the Selectmen of Stoughtonham, July 6, 1775; Cooke at 2.

[318] Letter from Joseph Reed to Samuel Garish, July 13, 1775.

[319] Robert K. Wright, *The Continental Army*, (Washington D.C.: Center of Military History, 1983), 29.

[320] *Ibid.* The Commander in chief also tackled other problems hindering the army. He established an administrative staff, logistical guidelines, medical procedures and field music. *Ibid* at 29 - 41.

personalities at Boston. As a result of Washington's actions, Gerrish's Regiment was reassigned to General Heath's Brigade, Major General Putnam's Division and was redesignated Colonel Gerrish's 38th Regiment of Foot.[321]

In late July, a British floating battery attacked the fortifications at Sewall's Point. Colonel Gerrish, commanding the position, made no attempt to repel the assault, arguing, "The rascals can do us no harm, and it would be a mere waste of powder to fire at them with our four-pounders."[322] As evening set in, he ordered the lights of the fortification extinguished. In the darkness, the British continued the bombardment, although the cannon balls flew wide of the fort.[323] For his conduct, Gerrish was immediately arrested. On August 18, 1775, he was tried at Harvard University in the College Chapel for "conduct unworthy of an officer."[324] The next day he was found guilty. As a result of the verdict, Washington ordered

> Col Samuel Garish of the Massachusetts Forces, tried by a General Court Martial of which Brigadier Genl. Green was Presdt. is unanimously found guilty of the Charge exhibited against him, *That he behaved unworthy an Officer*; that he is guilty of a Breach of the 49th Article of the Rules and Regulations of the Massachusetts Army. The Court therefore sentence and adjudge, the said Col Garish, to be cashiered, and render'd incapable of any employment in the American Army--The General approves the sentence of the Court martial, and orders it to take place immediately.[325]

---

[321] That same day, the regiment was ordered to protect Chelsea, Malden, Sewall's Point and Medford. *Massachusetts Soldiers and Sailors of the American Revolution*; George Washington, July 22, 1775, General Orders.

[322] Frothingham at 179.

[323] *Ibid.*

[324] George Washington, August 17, 1775, General Orders.

[325] George Washington, August 19, 1775, General Orders. Many officers, including the judge advocate presiding over the hearing, declared the

After Gerrish's removal, command of the regiment was turned over to its lieutenant colonel, Loammi Baldwin of Woburn. On April 19th, Baldwin had been one of the first militia officers to bring a force to the aid of Lexington, and to see the bloody results of the engagement on the common. Afterwards, he led two hundred Woburn militiamen against the retreating British, and devastated their lines at the Bloody Angle in Lincoln. Upon his assuming command in August, the regiment not only experienced a complete reversal from the plague of military blunders and mismanagement it had experienced previously, but quickly developed into one of the army's crack fighting units. Over the next year and a half, Baldwin would lead his regiment across Massachusetts, to New York, to Pennsylvania and New Jersey. In New York, the regiment fought like wolves in helping to hold off a British amphibious landing at Pelham Bay. The regiment later comprised a part of the force that crossed the Delaware River with General Washington on Christmas Night 1776 to route the Hessian garrison at Trenton, and an advance party of the regiment was given the honor of leading the march to Princeton. Baldwin proved not only a capable officer, but also an innovative engineer and agriculturist when, after the war, he designed the Middlesex Canal that connected the Charles and Merrimack rivers and developed the Baldwin apple.[326]

As the months of 1775 passed, the men of Wood's Company remained at their post in Chelsea. They continued, much to the anxiety of the local residents, to collect cattle for the army, while also maintaining a careful watch on the besieged garrison and the movements of ships in and out of Boston.[327] In the fall, the regimental dress took on a note of

---

punishment was too severe. Following his removal, Gerrish returned to Newbury. Despite his court-martial, the townsmen elected Gerrish to the General Court in 1776.

[326] Fischer at 288.

[327] During this time, Baldwin took it personally upon himself to ensure Washington was continuously apprised of all activity emanating from Boston. The general first learned of the erection of breastworks on Bunker

uniformity, when the men were issued tan and tobacco-brown colored bounty coats adorned with simple regimental buttons stamped with the number "38". In mid-November, Baldwin fretted "We are under some apprehension that the British . . . will pay us a visit."[328] The regiment braced itself for an amphibious assault from Boston that never came. On December 31, 1775, enlistments for the men in Wood's Company finally expired. Some Lexington men went home, but many more enlisted in the 12th and 26th Continental Regiments.

Hill by the British from Baldwin on September 15, 1775. On October 1, 1775, he assured Washington that the brief cannonade initiated by the British was to cover a party ordered to retrieve an officer's horse stranded on Noodle Island. The colonel even took it upon himself to inform Washington of any civilians crossing the siege lines by water from Boston. *See* Loammi Baldwin to George Washington, September 15, 1775; Loammi Baldwin to George Washington, October 1, 1775; and Loammi Baldwin to George Washington, August 2, 1775.

[328] Letter from Loammi Baldwin to his wife, November 14, 1775.

~8~

Conclusion: Name Among the Nations of the Earth

Throughout the war, one hundred and six men, including the slave Prince Estabrook, enlisted in the Continental Army and fought for the cause of independence from Canada, to New York, New Jersey, Pennsylvania and Virginia. Many died, but most returned home safely.

Those men who did not enlist were still obligated by law to serve in the town militia. In times of crisis, a certain percentage of men from each Massachusetts militia company were called upon to serve temporarily in militia regiments. Throughout the war, the Lexington Training Band not only served as a home guard, but between 1776 and 1781, over 150 men from the town volunteered and saw service at Long Island, Saratoga, Rhode Island, Penobscot Bay and New Bedford.

However, as the years passed, Lexington continued to suffer from the ravages of war, which now included the burdens of disease, food shortages and inflation. Within months of the commencement of the Siege of Boston, military hospitals were set up by American forces in Cambridge,

Watertown and Menotomy. Unfortunately, with a lack of effective quarantine regulations, camp fever, also known as typhus, spread from the American siege lines into the surrounding communities, including Lexington. This caused massive suffering and a rise in premature deaths, especially amongst children.

Lexington was also devastated economically during the war. Shortly after the Battles of Lexington and Concord, the Colony of Massachusetts began to issue paper currency to support its war effort. In January, 1777, the currency was worth approximately nineteen shillings. By December, 1778, it had depreciated to less than three shillings. Complicating matters was a widespread shortage of common goods and supplies, including rum, leather, cloth, beef and dairy products. This resulted in massive price inflation of supplies and services.

In response to the growing economic crisis, the Massachusetts government ordered in July, 1778 a convention to convene in Concord, Massachusetts. Matthew Mead, Thaddeus Parker and Joseph Viles served as representatives on behalf of Lexington. The convention recommended that the towns of Massachusetts adopt price fixing measures on most goods and services.

Lexington quickly adopted its own price fixing measures. The list generated not only established price control measures designed to combat inflation, but also revealed what were common goods and services in demand in Lexington during the Revolutionary War:

West India Rum, £6, 9s per gallon
New England Rum, £4, 16s per gallon
Molasses, £4, 15s per gallon
Coffee, 18s per pound
Brown Sugar, from 11s to 14s per pound
Chocolate, 24s per pound

Cotton Wool, 37s, 6d per pound
German Steel, 36s per pound
Indian Corn, £4, 4s per bushel
Salt, Best Quality, £10, 10s per bushel
Wheat, £8, 10s per bushel
Beef, from 3s to 4s, 6d per pound
Cyder, £5, 10d per barrel
Yard Wide Tow Cloth, 24s
Sole Leather, 20s per pound
Carpenter's or Mason's Work, 60s per day
West Indian Flip per Mug, 15s
Extraordy Good Dinner, 20s
Best Saddles, £60
Best Felt Hats, £4
Lodging, 4s[329]

Approximately six weeks before the signing of the Declaration of Independence in Philadelphia, the town was openly discussing a break from England. On May 23, 1776, the Town resolved "to refer the important matter . . . relating to the independency of the Colonies to the wisdom and prudence of that August assembly the Honorable Continental Congress . . . and if the said Congress should for the safety of these colonies declare them Independent of the Kingdom of Great Britain we stand ready with our Lives and Fortunes to support them in the measure."[330] When Massachusetts decided to draft its own constitution, Lexington immediately selected the Reverend Clarke as its delegate. As with before the war, Lexington remained on the cutting edge of the political spectrum.

In 1854, the last survivor of the Battle of Lexington, fifer Jonathan Harrington, died at the age of ninety-six. At his funeral, more American soldiers marched than had fought at

---

[329] Charles Hudson, History of the Town of Lexington, *Genealogies*, Vol. I, (Boston: Houghton Mifflin Company, 1913), 237.
[330] Declarations and Resolves, Town of Lexington, May 23, 1776.

Lexington and Concord seventy-nine years earlier. The last of those who had stood on Lexington Common that April morning in defense of liberty had now passed on. But they and the small New England town where the American Revolution began would always remain fresh in our collective memory having "given to us a name among the nations of the earth."[331]

---

[331] "A Sermon Preached Before His Excellency, John Hancock", Jonas Clarke, 1781.

APPENDIX A

THE LEXINGTON COMMON ON
APRIL 19, 1775

In review of the documentation on the Battle of
Lexington, particularly the depositions of the Lexington
militia men, it is probable that as the light infantry companies
of the 4th and 10th Foot stepped onto the village common, the
sun had yet to rise. Thomas Rice Willard watched the battle
from a window in Daniel Harrington's house, located at the
back of the Lexington common. Four days later, he testified
"On the Nineteenth instant, in the morning, about a half hour
before sunrise, I looked out at the window of said house, and
saw (as I suppose) about four hundred regulars in one Body."[332]
John Robbins noted the training band "being drawn up
(sometime before sun Rise) on the Green or Common . . .there
suddenly appear'd a Number of the Kings Troops."[333]
William Draper, a resident of Colrain, Massachusetts who
happened to be in Lexington on April 19th declared "about a
half hour before sunrise, the King's Regular Troops appeared
at the meeting house of Lexington."[334] Finally, Thomas
Fessenden asserted that as he stood in a pasture, he watched
the regulars enter the common and rush the training band "at
about half an hour before sunrise."[335]

Along with the darkness, the militiamen of the
Lexington Training Band were also in a state of confusion. As
the British advanced towards the common, Captain Parker
initially ordered his men to "Let the troops pass by, and don't

---

[332] Deposition of Thomas Rice Willard, April 23, 1775.
[333] Deposition of John Robbins, April 24, 1775.
[334] Deposition of William Draper, April 25, 1775.
[335] Deposition of Thomas Fessenden, April 23, 1775.

molest them, without they begin first."[336] However, when the light infantrymen rushed towards his company, Parker quickly reversed his own instructions. "I immediately ordered our militia to disperse, and not to fire."[337] Because of Parker's inconsistent commands, many, but not all, of the militiamen broke ranks and began to retire from the field. But simultaneously, additional men arrived at the parade ground to join the Lexington Training Band. Nathaniel Parkhurst affirmed, "we attended to the beat of our drum, and were formed on the Parade; we were faced towards the Regulars then marching up to us, and some of our Company were comeing to the parade with their backs towards the Troops, and Others on the parade, began to disperse when the Regulars fired on the Company."[338] According to Daniel Harrington, "Upon information being received . . . that the troops were not far off, the . . . company collected together . . . by the time the regulars appeared . . . [The company was] chiefly in a confused state and only a few of them being drawn up."[339] Within the space of minutes, the training band had become a confused mob.

The combination of the darkness, spectators gathered in small clusters and militiamen coming and going from the common must have contributed to Major Pitcairn and Lieutenant Sutherland's false impression that a large number of armed provincials were drawn up on the Lexington Common. One officer believed he saw two militia companies formed on the common. Ensign Henry De Berniere of the 10th Foot, described the Lexington men drawn up in two "divisions", with a company-wide space between the two.[340]

---

[336] Deposition of Paul Revere, April 24, 1775.
[337] Deposition of John Parker, April 25, 1775.
[338] Deposition of Nathaniel Parkhurst, April 25, 1775.
[339] *An account of the commencement of Hostilities between Great Britain and America, in the Province of the Massachusetts-Bay. By the Reverend Mr. William Gordon of Roxbury, in a Letter to a Gentlemen in England, dated May 17, 1775.*
[340] Henry De Berniere, *Narrative of Occurrences, 1775*, (Boston, 1779).

126

Naturally, this begs the question: is it possible that there were two companies of Lexington militia on the common on April 19th?

Daniel Harrington, almost a month after the battle, reported that when the militia mustered earlier in the morning, "the train band or Militia, and the alarm men (consisting of the aged and others exempted from turning out, excepting upon alarm) repaired in general to the common, close in with the meeting-house, the usual place of parade; and there were present when the roll was called over about one hundred and thirty of both."[341] Yet, Harrington is silent as to whether the alarm list and training band mustered together or as separate companies. When the militia assembled for a second time, there is no reference by Harrington to a second company and those who mustered are merely described as "the remains of the company."[342] Likewise, not a single deposition signed by spectators and Lexington militiamen makes reference to more than one company mustering on the field.

However, loyalist and Boston resident George Leonard, who accompanied Percy's relief column as a scout, indirectly suggested in his deposition that *another* company, perhaps unattached to the Lexington Company, was responsible for the first shot at the Battle of Lexington. "That being on horseback . . .he several times went forward of the Brigade; in one of which excursions he met with a Countryman who was wounded supported by two others who were armed . . .the Deponent then asked what provoked [the regulars] to do it . . . he said that Some of our people upon the Regulars . . . he said further that it was not the Company he belonged to that fired but some of our Country people that were on the other Side of the Road."[343] Nevertheless, Leonard's deposition is in direct contradiction with a

---

[341] Gordon, "An account of the commencement of Hostilities . . ."
[342] *Ibid.*
[343] Deposition of George Leonard, May 4, 1775.

statement given by James Marr of the 4th Foot to the
Reverend William Gordon. According to Marr, "when they
and the others were advanced, Major Pitcairn said to the
Lexington Company, (which, by the by, was the only one
there), stop, you rebels! And he supposed that the design was
to take away their arms."[344]

It is entirely possible that Captain Parker had
organized his rather large company into four platoons or
"divisions". If this were the case, it would be likely that
Parker and the Lexington Training Band would have used the
Norfolk Drill. The drill instructs officers of companies with
more than forty men to divide the company into four divisions,
"in which case the captain leads the first, and the ensign the
third, the lieutenant bringing up the rear. In general, the rule
is, that the chief or commanding officer leads the whole, the
second in command brings up the rear and the others lead the
intermediate divisions."[345]

Thus, the observations of De Berniere could have been
of either the remnants of the Lexington Training Band as
described by Harrington or an incomplete company that was
simultaneously dispersing and falling in as the British
advanced. Unfortunately, no evidence exists as to what drill
the training band utilized and as a result, what De Berniere
observed remains a mystery.

---

[344] Gordon, "An account of the commencement of Hostilities . . ."
[345] George Townshend, A Plan of Discipline Composed for the Use of the
Militia of the County of Norfolk, (London, 1759), 44, n.2.

APPENDIX B

BRITISH CASUALTIES SUSTAINED DURING THE BATTLES OF LEXINGTON AND CONCORD[346]

A. British Officers

Regiment	Name
4th Regiment	Lt. Gould, wounded in foot
	Lt. Hackshaw, wounded in cheek
	Lt. Cox, wounded in arm
10th Regiment	Lt. Col Smith, wounded in leg
	Capt. Parsons, wounded in knee
	Lt. Kelly, wounded in arm
	Ensign Lister, wounded in arm
23rd Regiment	Lt. Col Bernard, wounded in thigh
38th Regiment	Lt. Sutherland, wounded in chest

[346] Source: Diary of Lt. Frederick Mackenzie, April 19, 1775.

43rd Regiment	Lt Hall, wounded in chest, died May 2, 1775
47th Regiment	Lt. McLeod, wounded in chest
	Lt. Baldwin, wounded in throat
Marines	Captain Souter, wounded in leg
	Lt. McDonald, wounded slightly
	Lt. Dotter, wounded slightly

B. Enlisted Men

Regiment	KIA	WIA	MIA
4th	7	25	8
5th	5	15	1
10th	1	13	1
18th	1	4	1
23rd	4	26	6
38th	4	12	0
43rd	4	5	2
47th	5	22	0
52nd	3	2	1
59th	3	3	0
Marines	31	38	2
Artillery	0	2	0

APPENDIX C

PROVINCIAL CASUALTIES SUSTAINED DURING THE BATTLES OF LEXINGTON AND CONCORD[347]

Militia Company	KIA	WIA	MIA
Lexington	10	9	0
Menotomy	3	1	2
Sudbury	2	1	0
Concord	1	6	0
Bedford	1	1	0
Acton	3	2	0
Woburn	2	3	0
Charlestown	1	0	0
Brookline	1	0	0
Cambridge	3	0	2
Medford	2	1	0
Lynn	4	2	1
Danvers	7	2	1
Salem	1	0	0
Framingham	0	1	0

---

[347] Source: "A Narrative of the Excursion and Ravages of the King's Troops Under the Command of general Gage on the Nineteenth of April, 1775."

Beverly	1	3	0
Watertown	1	0	0
Newton	0	1	0
Billerica	0	2	0
Chelmsford	0	2	0
Stow	0	1	0
Dedham	1	1	0
Needham	5	2	0
Roxbury	0	0	1
Lincoln	0	1	0

APPENDIX D

RANKING OF MASSACHUSETTS MINUTE AND MILITIA COMPANIES BY CASUALTIES SUSTAINED

1.	**Lexington**	19 casualties sustained
2.	**Danvers**	10 casualties sustained
3.	**Concord**	7 casualties sustained
	Lynn	7 casualties Sustained
	Needham	7 casualties sustained
4.	**Menotomy**	6 casualties sustained
5.	**Acton**	5 casualties sustained
	Woburn	5 casualties sustained
	Cambridge	5 casualties sustained
6.	**Beverly**	4 casualties sustained
7.	**Sudbury**	3 casualties sustained
	Medford	3 casualties sustained
8.	**Bedford**	2 casualties sustained
	Billerica	2 casualties sustained
	Chelmsford	2 casualties sustained
	Dedham	2 casualties sustained
9.	**Charlestown**	1 casualty sustained

Brookline	1 casualty sustained
Salem	1 casualty sustained
Framingham	1 casualty sustained
Watertown	1 casualty sustained
Newton	1 casualty sustained
Stow	1 casualty sustained
Roxbury	1 casualty sustained
Lincoln	1 casualty sustained

APPENDIX E

MEMBERS OF THE LEXINGTON TRAINING BAND
PRESENT AT THE BATTLE OF LEXINGTON[348]

Captain Parker's Company had a roster of 144 men. Seventy-seven members stood on the Common on the morning of April 19, 1775 in defiance of the King's orders to "lay down your arms". Those men included:

Captain John Parker	Lt. William Tidd
Ensign Robert Monroe	Ensign Joseph Simonds
Clerk: Daniel Harrington	Cpl. John Munroe
Cpl. Joel Viles	Cpl. Samuel Sanderson
Orderly Sgt. William Munroe	Cpl Ebenezer Parker
Solomon Brown	Ebenezer Bowman
John Bridge, Jr.	James Brown
John Brown	Jonathan Harrington (Fifer)
John Chandler	John Chandler, Jr.
Joseph Comee	Robert Douglass
Isaac Durant	Nathaniel Farmer
Isaac Green	
William Grimes	Caleb Harrington
John Harrington	Jonathan Harrington, Jr.
Moses Harrington, 3rd	Moses Harrington, Jr.

---

[348] Source: http://people.ne.mediaone.net/wrcmc/Roster.html. The Official Web Site for the Lexington Minute Men, Inc.

Thaddeus Harrington	Thomas Harrington
Isaasc Hastings	Samuel Hastings
Samuel Hadley	Thomas Hadley, Jr.
Micah Hagar	Amos Lock
Benjamin Lock	Reuben Lock
Abner Mead	Ebenezer Munroe
Jedediah Munroe	John Munroe, Jr.
Nathan Munroe	William Munroe, 3rd
Nathaniel Mulliken	Isaac Muzzy
John Muzzy	Jonas Parker
Jonas Parker, Jr.	Nathaniel Parkhurst
Solomon Pierce	Asahel Porter (prisoner)
Joshua Reed	Joshua Reed, Jr.
Nathan Reed	John Robbins
Phillip Russell	Benjamin Sampson
Joshua Simonds	John Smith
Phineas Smith	Simeon Snow
Phineas Stearns	Jonas Stone, Jr.
John Tidd	Joseph Underwood
Benjamin Wellington	Sylvanus Wood
John Winship	Thomas Winship
Enoch Wellington	James Wyman

APPENDIX F

PROPRTY DAMAGE OF LEXINGTON HOMES ALONG THE ROUTE OF PERCY'S RETREAT FROM LEXINGTON TO BOSTON

1. Deacon Joseph Loring   £720

2. Matthew Mead   £101

3. Benjamin Merriam   £223, 4s

4. Lydia Mulliken   £431

5. Joshua Bond   £189, 16s, 7d

6. William Munroe   £203, 11s, 9d

7. John Mason   £14, 13s, 4d

APPENDIX G

EQUIPMENT OF MASSACHUSETTS MILITIA AND MINUTE MEN IN THE 18TH CENTURY

Unlike the British counterpart, there was no uniform issuance of equipment. Militia men of Massachusetts acquired their weapons from a variety of sources: inheritance, the French and Indian War, the Siege of Louisbourg and from willing British soldiers stationed in Boston. However, throughout the colony's history, Massachusetts towns made some attempts to bring some semblance of uniformity to its militia companies. Militia laws and resolves were passed, although often with little success. The end result was a widespread mixture of French, British and American weapons and equipment.

Below are various accounts, regulations and laws regarding the use of militia weapons and equipment.

1. "Each soldier to provide himself with a good fire arm, a steel or iron ram rod and a spring for same, a worm, a priming wire and brush, a bayonet fitted to his gun, a scabbard and belt thereof, a cutting sword or tomahawk or hatchet, a . . .cartridge box holding fifteen rounds . . . at least, a hundred buckshot, six flints, one pound of powder, forty leaden balls fitted to the gun, a knapsack and blanket, [and] a canteen or wooden bottle to hold one quart [of water]" (*Journal of Arthur Harris of the Bridgewater Coy of Militia*)

2. "A firelock, bayonet, waistbelt, a cartridge box, cartridges, and a knapsack." (*An Easy Plan of Discipline for a Militia*, Timothy Pickering, p. 1-4)

3. "Militia minutemen [who were to] hold themselves in readiness at a minutes warning, compleat in arms and ammunition; that is to say a good and sufficient firelock, bayonet, thirty rounds of powder and ball, pouch and knapsack." (*Town of Roxbury Resolves,* December 26, 1774)

4. "The Third Bristol County Militia Regiment wanted their men to have the following at muster: "a good firearm with steel or iron ramrod, and spring to retain the same, a worm, priming wire and brush, and a bayonet fitted to his gun, a tomahawk or hatchet, a pouch containing a cartridge box that will hold fifteen rounds of cartridges at least, a hundred of buckshot, a jack knife, and tow for wadding, six flints, one pound of powder, forty leaden balls fitted to his gun, a knapsack and blanket, a canteen or wooden bottle sufficient to hold one quart." (*Continental Journal and Weekly Adviser,* January 22, 1778.)

5. Another early company document mentions "a powder horn, a bullet pouch to contain 40 leaden balls, a knapsack, a canteen, a firearm of good worth, a haversack, a belt, a good pair of overalls." (*Boston Gazette* May 26, 1777)

6. "List of Men & accouterments of Each man [illegible words] Regiment in Bristol County [Massachusetts]" from private collection. Dated 1776: "Men including officers - 678, Firearms - 446, Ramrods - 129, Springs - 9, Worms - 160, Priming wires - 193, Brushes - 138, Bayonets - 175, Scabbards - 142, Belts - 181, Cutting swords & hatchets - 255, Cartridge box and powder - 274, Buckshot - 10373, Jackknives - 403, Tow for men – 258, flints for men - 2084, pounds powder - 244 1/2, Bullets - 11934, Knapsack - 365, Blankets - 386, Canteens - 295"

7. Massachusetts militia men were required to fall out with "his firelock in good repair, four pounds of lead in bullets, fitted to the bore of his piece, four flints, a cutlass or

tomahawk, a good belt round his body, a canvas knapsack to hold a bushel, with a good matumpline, fitting easy across the breast and shoulders, good clothing, etc." (*Source undated and unknown, but original shown to Henry Cooke by Peter Oakley in 1995*)

8. The Town of Braintree required each soldier furnish himself with "a good fire lock, bayonett, cartouch box, one pound of powder, twenty-four balls to fitt their guns, twelve flints and a knapsack." (*Town of Braintree Resolves*, January 23, 1775)

9. As militiamen from the village of Lynn marched off to war on April 19, 1775, an observer noted "[one man with] a long fowling piece, without a bayonet, a horn of powder, and a seal-skin pouch, filled with bullets and buckshot. . . Here an old soldier carried a heavy Queen's arm with which he had done service at the conquest of Canada twenty years previous, while by his side walked a stripling boy with a Spanish fusee not half its weight or calibre, which his grandfather may have taken at the Havana, while not a few had old French pieces, that dated back to the reduction of Louisbourg." (*History of Lynn*, p. 338)

10. Massachusetts provincial soldiers were issued the following items throughout the French and Indian War: "Canteen, Wooden bottle one hoop" (Massachusetts Historical Society, *Journal of the House of Representatives*, vol. 35, p. 287 and 335); "Knapsacks" (Acts and Resolves, Public and Private, of the Province of the Massachusetts-Bay, p. 313); "Arms and Cartridge Boxes" (*Diary Kept at Louisbourg, 1759-1760, by Jonathan Procter of Danvers*, p. 70)

11. "To be sold by John Pim of Boston, Gunsmith, at the Sign of the Cross Guns, in Anne-Street near the Draw Bridge, at very Reasonable rates, sundry choice of Arms lately arrived from London, viz. Handy Muskets, Buccaneer-Guns, Fowling Pieces, Hunting Guns, Carbines, several sorts of Pistols, Brass

and Iron, fashionable swords, &c." (*Boston Newsletter*, July 11, 1720)

12. "Newly imported, and sold by Samuel Miller, Gunsmith, at the Sign of the Cross Guns near the Draw-Bridge, Boston: Neat Fire Arms of all sorts, Pistols, Swords, Hangars, Cutlasses, Flasks for Horsemen, Firelocks, &c." (*Boston Gazette*, May 11, 1742)

13. "Every listed souldier ... shall be alwayes provided with a well fixt firelock musket, of musket or bastard musket bore, the barrel not less then three foot and a half long, or other good firearms to the satisfaction of the commission officers of the company, a snapsack, a coller with twelve bandeleers or cartouch-box, one pound of good powder, twenty bullets fit for his gun, and twelve flints, a good sword or cutlace, a worm and priming wire fit for his gun" (*Mass. Militia Laws,* Nov. 22, 1693)

14. "Every soldyer Shall be well provided w'th a well fixed gun or fuse, Sword or hatchet, Snapsack, Catouch box, horne Charger & flints" (*New Hampshire Militia Laws,* Oct. 7, 1692)

15. "We killed and took about the same number of the enemy. The lieuttenant of the British company and myself, were foremost, and we advanced on and found their sleeping-place, and while running it up, the Lieutenant was shot through the vitals and he died soon thereafter. Thus I was all alone, the remainder of our party not having gained the summit; the enemy retreated, and i followed them to the other end of the hill. In my route on the hill, I picked up a good French gun and brought it home with me." (*The Life of Captain David Perry, A Soldier of the French and Revolutionary Wars*)

16. ". . . before I arrived at Concord I see one of the grenadiers standing sentinel. I cocked my piece and run up to him, seized his gun with my left hand. He surrender his armor, one gun and bayonet, a large cutlash [cutlass] and brass

fender, one box over the shoulder with twenty-two rounds, one box round the waist with eighteen rounds." (*Pension application of Sylvanus Wood, a Massachusetts militiaman who captured a British grenadier on April 19, 1775*)

17. Equipment lost at Bunkerhill by the men of Captain Currier's Company, Colonel Frye's Regiment: 4 muskets, 5 coats, 5 blankets, 3 greatcoats, 9 snapsacks, 1 pair of shoes, 2 pairs of socks, 1 hat, 1 pair of "trowsers" and two neckerchiefs. (*History of Amesbury and Merrimac*)

18. "Every listed Soldier, and other Householder shall be always provided with a well fixt Firelock Musket, of Musket or Bastard-Musket bore, the Barrel not less than three Foot and an half long, or other good Fire Arms to the satisfaction of the Commission Officers of the Company; a Cartouch Box: one Pound of good Powder: Twenty Bullets fit for his Gun, and twelve Flynts; a good Sword or Cutlass; a Worm, & priming Wire, fit for his Gun, on Penalty of six Shillings..." (*Boston Newsletter*, February 7, 1733)

19. "A proportion of Ordnance and stores for the intended expedition to North America

By order of the Board dated the 12th of October 1754 . . . For Service of the two American Regiments . . . Musquets with Bayonets with Nosebands & wood rammers: 1000 . . . Dutch with nosebands & wood R.: 1000 . . . Cartouch Boxes with Straps [and] 12 Holes: 2000 . . . Swords with Scabbards with Brass Hilts: 320 . . . with Iron Hilts: 1800 . . .Halberts: 80."[349] (*Braddock's Orderly Books,* May 12th, 1755; *Military Affairs in North America*)

20. "Return of the Arms & Accoutrements of the following Corps, Lost, and Broke, on the 19th April 1775 . . .Firelocks

---

[349] Although these items were not issued to Massachusetts Provincial Regiments, it is an example of the possible weapons issued to Massachusetts soldiers.

lost: 97 . . . Bayonets lost: 143 . . . Swords lost: 4 . . . Pouches
with shoulder belts lost: 43 . . . Waist belts lost: 52 . . . Slings
lost: 70 . . . Cartridge Boxes lost: 10 . . . Sword scabbards lost:
4 . . . Bayonet scabbards lost: 27 . . . Match cases lost: 3."
(*List of muskets and equipment lost by the 4th, 5th, 10th, 18th,
23rd, 38th, 43rd, 47th, 52nd, 59th Regiments and Marines.*
Source: WO 36/3, PRO)

21. "In the name of God amen. On this Eleventh day of
December AnnoDom 1754. I Daniel Kimball of Andover in ye
county of Essex in the Province of ye Massachusetts Bay in
New England, yeoman being Indisposed in Body but of
Perfect mind and memory and calling to mind my mortality do
make and ordain this my last will and testimony (viz) first of
all I remand my soul unto the hands of God that Gave it and
my Body I Comend to the Earth to be Decently Buried at ye
Descretion of my Executors hereafter named. Expecting and
Believing ye Resurection of ye same at ye last day--- and as
Touching such worldly Estate as hathe pleased almighty God
to Confer upon me. I give & Dispose of it in ye following
maner I(illegible) I will that my just Debt and funeral Expense
shall be truly and fairly paid in convenient time after my
decease by my Executors hereafter named Item . . . I give and
Bequethe to my said son Andrew all my stock of Brutual
Creture of Every Name & Kind Together with all my
husbandry tools & Tackling Shop & Coopers Tools also all
my Barrel tub rags, Sword, gun, pistol Holster, Saddle &
Grate Bible" (*Estate of Daniel Kimball of Andover,
Massachusetts Bay Colony,* December 11, 1754)

22. "An Inventory of the Estate of Caleb Coy, late of
Wenham, post-oath on by us the said subscribers this thirtieth
day of November, Seventeen Hundred and Fifty Four in
lawfull money: One large flintlock & armour (1lb, 6s, 8d) and
one other flintlock £2 10s 4d." (*Estate of Caleb Coy of
Wenham, Massachusetts Bay Colony,* November 13, 1754)

23. "The following names are a full and Just account of those to whom I the Subscriber delivered Bayonets in the company under my command in Lexington, Benjamin Reed, Captain, June 5, 1759... [49 militia men listed]" (Massachusetts Muster Rolls, Volume 97, Page 216)

APPENDIX H

AN OVERVIEW OF PRE-REVOLUTIONARY WAR
CARTRIDGE BOXES

In the spring of 1775, Massachusetts residents
struggled to equip its fledgling provincial army. One problem
the Committee of Safety recognized was the need to properly
carry bullet rounds, commonly referred to as cartridges.
Although hunting pouches were commonplace among
Massachusetts soldiers, A short review of Massachusetts
militia laws and resolves on the eve of Lexington and Concord
reveals the urgency for the adoption of cartridge boxes.[350] Yet
by 1776, the results were discouraging. For example, of the
678 men and officers in a Bristol County militia regiment,
only a mere 274 men had obtained cartridge boxes.[351]

---

[350] "Each soldier to provide himself with a good fire arm, a steel or iron
ram rod and a spring for same, a worm, a priming wire and brush, a
bayonet fitted to his gun, a scabbard and belt thereof, a cutting sword or
tomahawk or hatchet, a . . .cartridge box holding fifteen rounds . . . at least,
a hundred buckshot, six flints, one pound of powder, forty leaden balls
fitted to the gun, a knapsack and blanket, [and] a canteen or wooden bottle
to hold one quart [of water]" Journal of Arthur Harris of the Bridgewater
Coy of Militia.; "Militia minutemen [who were to] hold themselves in
readiness at a minutes warning, compleat in arms and ammunition; that is
to say a good and sufficient firelock, bayonet, thirty rounds of powder and
ball, pouch and knapsack." Town of Roxbury Resolves, December 26,
1774; The Town of Braintree required each soldier furnish himself with "a
good fire lock, bayonet, cartouch box, one pound of powder, twenty-four
balls to fitt their guns, twelve flints and a knapsack." Town of Braintree
Resolves, January 23, 1775.
[351] "List of Men & accouterments of Each man [illegible words] Regiment
in Bristol County [Massachusetts]" from private collection. Dated 1776:
"Men including officers - 678, Firearms - 446, Ramrods - 129, Springs - 9,
Worms - 160, Priming wires - 193, Brushes - 138, Bayonets - 175,
Scabbards - 142, Belts - 181, Cutting swords & hatchets - 255, Cartridge
box and powder - 274, Buckshot - 10373, Jackknives - 403, Tow for men -
258 flints for men - 2084, pounds powder - 244 1/2, Bullets - 11934,
Knapsack - 365, Blankets - 386, Canteens - 295".

In light of this attempt, the question arises what did these boxes look like? Naturally, the design varied from maker to maker. A box from the Siege of Louisbourg varied from a Massachusetts box made for the 1759 campaign against the French. Yet, in light of these differences, the more important question is, given the accuracy of smooth-bore muskets, the intended purpose of a socket bayonet and the shortage of such edged weapons within the Massachusetts army, of those boxes that were present on April 19th, how many rounds did these boxes contain?

It appears that the number of rounds a cartridge box could hold varied from box to box. According to the Reverend Samuel Chandler, the French cartridge boxes he observed during the French and Indian War contained "3 rows, 10 in a row, 30 cartridges and 30 bullets lose."[352] The list of stores for General Braddock's expedition, dated October 12, 1754, revealed "For service of the two Irish Regiments: . . . Cartouch Boxes with Straps . . .12 holes . . . 1400:; "For service of the Two American Regiments: Cartouch Boxes with straps . . .12 holes . . . 2000."[353] In a letter of Henry Bouquet to Forbes, dated June 14, 1758, the author notes, "I have noticed a great inconvenience in the use of cartridge boxes for the provincial troops. They do not know how to make cartridges, or rather, they take too much time. In the woods, they seldom have time or places suitable to make them. These cartridge boxes hold only 9 charges, some twelve, which is not sufficient. I think that their powder horns and pouches would be more useful, keeping the cartridge box, however, to use in case of a sudden or night attack."[354]

---

[352] "Extracts from the Diary of Rev. Samuel Chandler . . ." New *England Historical Genealogical Register,* Vol. XVII (1863), p. 346-354.
[353] Stanley Pargellis, "Military Affairs in North America 1748-1765: Selected Documents from the Cumberland Papers in Windsor Castle, p. 486 (1936), p. 2.
[354] "The Papers of Henry Bouquet", Vol. II, p. 88.

Artifacts recovered from the British man-of-war
Invincible, wrecked in the Solent while sailing for the invasion
of Louisbourg in 1758, also provide detailed information
about cartridge boxes. Among the items recovered in 1979
was a nine-hole belly box with part of the leather flap still
intact.[355] In the "General Orders of 1757 Issued by the Earl of
Loudoun and Phineas Lyman in the Campaign Against the
French", the orders indicate effective "July 2d, 1757, at Fort
Edward, that Each Man be provided with 24 Rounds of
Powder & Ball." In 1758, the amount of ammunition carried
was increased to 36 rounds as found in Montpenny's Orderly
Book. On September 17, 1758, the "Brigade Major (was) to
review the men for duty dayly on the parade before they
mount Guard & see that they have their blankets & provisions,
& also 36 rounds of ammunition."

Provincial boxes also varied on the eve of Lexington
and Concord. A belly box recovered in Middlesex County had
twelve rounds with an additional seven added when a second
block was nailed to the first.[356] Another box unearthed in
Southern Massachusetts had 23 rounds,[357] while a box on
display at Fort Ticonderoga had 24 rounds.[358]

Militia laws and resolves also provided some insight
into how many rounds a cartridge box should have, although it
appears a *minimum* number was left undecided. The Town of
Bridgewater expected its soldiers to be equipped with a
"pouch containing a cartridge box that will hold fifteen rounds
of cartridges, *at least*."[359] Roxbury required every militia and
minuteman to carry "thirty rounds of gunpowder and ball."[360]

---

[355] The flap has a GR cipher and could have belonged to either a marine or
one of the invasion forces. For a detailed color picture, see Brian Lavery,
"The Royal Navy's First Invincible", pp. ix, 70 (1988).

[356] This box may be viewed at Minute Man National Historical Park,
Concord, Massachusetts.

[357] Neumann, 68.

[358] *Ibid*, 74.

[359] Journal of Arthur Harris of Bridgewater. (Emphasis added)

When Massachusetts adopted Timothy Pickering's drill in 1776, the number of rounds for a cartridge box was never addressed.[361]

Clearly, the variety of cartridge box rounds posed a problem for Massachusetts militia on April 19, 1775. However, as Lt. William Sutherland recalled, "[The] fire now *never slackened* . . .as we left Concord, but always found it heavier . . . where we saw these partys upon the heights."[362] Whether the heavy and constant fire was attributable to the number of militiamen on the field, the supplementing of cartridge boxes with pouches or both is an issue that remains to be unresolved.

---

[360] Town Resolve of Roxbury, December 26, 1774.
[361] One may argue this is evidence of the variety of cartridge boxes and their number of rounds within the colony.
[362] Report of Lieutenant William Sutherland to Major Kemble, April 27, 1775.

APPENDIX I

EXAMPLES OF MIDDLE AND LOWER CLASS MALE DRESS IN 18TH CENTURY MASSACHUSETTS

The following collection of runaway and merchant advertisements has been compiled in order to illustrate the common materials, patterns and fabrics of 18th century men's clothing available on the eve of the American Revolution. Examples include, but are not limited to, descriptions of hats and caps, jackets, trousers, shoes and breeches.

A. Hats and Caps

1.   "Ran away from me the Subscriber, on the 4th instant, an apprentice Lad named Uriah Stone, about 18 years of Age; he is Short in Stature, and of a dark Complexion. He had on when he went away a Flannel Jacket without Sleeves, a striped Tow Shirt, a Pair of Short Wide Trowsers, and an Old Felt Hat. Whoever Apprehends said Lad and brings him to his Master Sall be resonably rewarded for their Trouble. NATHANIEL BROWN Rehoboth, August 13, 1767."
   Providence Gazette, August 15, 1767

2. "DESERTED from Capt. Abimeleck Rigg's Company, in Colonel Talman's Regiment, Benjamin Wood, belonging to Norton, about 5 Feet 9 Inches high, somewhat slim built, of a dark Complexion, has short brown hair; had on when he went away a round Felt Hat, short grey Coat, Jacket and Breeches. Whoever will take up said Deserter, and secure him in any Gaol, or return him

to his Company, shall have Five Dollars Reward, and all necessary Charges, paid by ABIMELECK RIGGS, Capt." *Providence Gazette*, Feburary 8, 1777.

3. "Ran-away from his Master Edward Bardin, a Negro Man named Cuffe, about 22 years of Age, a tall Fellow his Legs crooked the small of them bending out, talks good English : Had on when he went away a white cloth Jacket, short skirts, a red Waistcoat under it, white Shirt, his Hat with a Gold wash'd Loop and Button, he formerly lived with Issac Winslow, Esq; of Roxbury, Whoever apprehends said Negro, and will bring him to his said Master living at the King's Arms on Boston Neck, shall have a Dollar Reward , and all necessary Charges paid. All Masters of Vessels and other are heredy cautioned against harbouring, concealing or carrying off said Servant as they would avoid the Penalty of the Law. Edward Bardin." *Boston News Letter,* December 28, 1769.

4. "RUN away from the subscriber, a Negro lad, named Pero, a smart well built fellow, about 15 years of age, speaks pretty good English, had on a great coat and straight bodied coat, of a brownish grey color, jacket and breeches of a colour somewhat different, home made, greyish stockings, a felt hat almost new, and a fulled cap. Whoever returns said Negro to me, shall have ten dollars reward, and necessary charges. OBADIAH READ. Rehoboth, Dec. 26, 1777." *Providence Gazette*, December 27, 1777.

5. "Ten Dollar Reward. RAN AWAY from the
Subscriber, Joseph Moors, of Groton, in the
County of Middlesex, and Province of
Massachusetts-Bay, a Malatto Man Servant, names
TITUS, sbout 20 Years of Age, of a middling
Statue, wears, short curl'd Hair, has one of his Fore
Teeth broke out, took with his a blue Surdan, a
Snuff coulor'd Coat, and a Pair, of white wash'd
Leather Breeches, a Pair of new Cow-hide Pumps,
and a Fur'd Hat with large Brims, and sundry other
Articles of Wearing Apparel.---Whoever will take
of said Servant and confine him in any of his
Majesty's Goals ....Joseph Moors." *Boston
Gazette,* July 25, 1774.

6. "FOUR DOLLARS REWARD. Ran-away from
the Subscriber on the 22d of September, at Night a
Negro Man Servant, by the Name of CATO, about
Five Feet and Eight Inches high, very thick Lips,
speaks broken, and Walks as if he was lame in his
Heels. Had on when he went away, a Cloth
colour'd Coat, with Pewter Buttons, old Leather
Breeches, a Tow Shirt, old Shoes with Silver plate
Buckles, wore a Cap, and ?hoves round his Neck,
and very high on his Forehead: Carried away with
him a Callico Banyan, fine Linen Shirt, Check
Linen Trowsers, grey Wigg, also carries or Wears a
Felt Hatt with a Silver Lace on it, had a Violin and
carries it in a green Bays Bag. Whosoever will
return the Runaway to his Master in Winchenden,
shall have the above Reward and all necessary
Charges, paid by LEVI NICHOL, Winchenden,

Sept. 23, 1774." *Boston Gazette*, Monday, October 10, 1774.

7.   "Joseph Peirce HAS IMPORTED by Captain SYMMES,(who is just arrived from LONDON) and is now opening at his Shop in Kings Street, nearly opposite the North Door of the Town-House, BOSTON . . .Mens white Beaver Hats." *Boston Gazette*, May 2, 1774.

B. Shirts

1.   "Ran away from me the Subscriber, on the 4th instant, an apprentice Lad named Uriah Stone, about 18 years of Age; he is Short in Stature, and of a dark Complexion. He had on when he went away a Flannel Jacket without Sleeves, a striped Tow Shirt, a Pair of Short Wide Trowsers, and an Old Felt Hat. Whoever Apprehends said Lad and brings him to his Master Shall be resonably rewarded for their Trouble. NATHANIEL BROWN Rehoboth, August 13, 1767." *Providence Gazette,* August 15, 1767.

2.   "Run away from the Subscriber, at Attleborough, on the 25th of July, a Lad about 17 years old, named Issac Allen, a thick chunky Fellow, about five Feet six Inches high, of a pale swarthy Complexion, has dark brown Hair, which he sometimes wears ty'd: Had on and took with him, when he went away, two Tow Shirts, one Check Linnen Ditto, a Pair of short wide Trowsers, a striped Flannel Jacket, a black Ditto, a yellow doubled and twisted Coat, two Hats, a Black Barcelona handkerchief, a Pair of Check Linen

Trowsers, two Pair of Stockings, and one Pair of
new Shoes. Whoever takes up said Runaway, and
brings him to his Master, shall have Two Dollars
Reward, and all necessary Charges, paid by me.
JOHN FISHER." *Providence Gazette*, Aug. 3,
1771.

3. "Run away from the Subscriber, the Night of the
    5th of April last, an Apprentice Lad, named Danile
    Bowen, about 20 years of Age, about 5 feet and a
    Half high, has brown Hair, grey eyes, is something
    round Shouldered, and understands making
    Buckles; Had on when he went away a new Felt
    Hat, a blue double breasted Jacket, with flowered
    Pewter Buttons, striped underflannel Jacket,
    Striped Flannel Shirt, Leather Breeches, and Yarn
    Stockings. Whoever takes up said Runaway, and
    brings him to his Master, Shall have Two Dollars
    Reward, and all necessary Charges, paid by
    BENJAMIN KINGSLEY. Rehoboth, April 25,
    1772." *Providence Gazette*, April 25, 1772.

4. "Ran-away from the Subscriber, living in Gorham,
    which joins Falmouth, Cumberland County in the
    Massachusetts Province, short Negro Man named
    Prince, about 26 Years of Age, 5 Feet some Inches
    high, talks broken English, has remarkable small
    Ears, and a Jewel Hole in one of them. Had on
    almost new Felt Hat, a reddish grey home-made
    Cloth Coat Jacket and Breeches, with silk knee
    Garters, a dark Callicoe under Jacket, a white
    Linnen Shirt, red Collar and Cuffs, to his Coat with
    Metal Buttons, white Cotton Stockings, Cald-Skin

Pumps,. It may be he has a Pass. Said Negro plays tolerable well on a Violin. Whosever will take up said Negro or bring him to his Master shall have Sixteen Dollars Reward, and all Charges paid by WILLIAM M'LEENEN." *Boston Gazette*, June 6, 1774.

5. "Stop Thief and Runaway Man Servant. Whereas William Hayward, Baker, absconded himself from my Service 16th March, 1774, and took with him to the Value of eight pounds , L. M. and be being taken and convicted, voluntarily Bound himself, to serve me Six Months, to Pay Damages & Cost: and he last Night absconded himself again; had on an old Felt Hat, an old cloth colour'd Coat and Waistcoat, check'd Woolen Shirt, a Pair of new cloth colour'd Breeches, a Pair of old pale blue Stockings, and a Pair of singleSole Shoes.--Said Hayward is about Thirty-three Years of Age, Five Feet Five Inches high, darkish, short Hair, and down look like a Rogue and Thief.----Whossoever will take up said Servant and Notify me the Subscriber so that I may have him again, shall have FIVE DOLLARS reward. Paid by me, ISAAC SHERMAN, Marlboro April 9, 1774. All Bakers are hereby cautioned against Employing said Servant." *Boston Gazette*, May 9, 1774.

C. Jackets and "Under Jackets"

1. "Rehoboth, August 12, 1763, Runaway from his master, Samuel Whitman, of Rehoboth, on Monday the 25th of July, an Apprentice Lad, about 17 years of age, named Edward Green, a Shoemaker by

trade. Had on when he went away, a blue coat, green Jacket, a light coloured pair of breeches, and wore his own hair: He is a short, thick fellow. Whoever takes up said lad, and returns him to his Master, or secures him in any of his Majesty's Gaols, so that he may be had again, shall receive THREE DOLLARS Reward, and all necessary Charges paid, by, SAMUEL WHITMANN.B. All Masters of Vessels and others are forewarned either secreting or carring off said Fellow, as they would avoid the Penalty of the Law." *Providence Gazette*, August 13, 1763.

2. "Run away from the Subscriber, at Attleborough, on the 25th of July, a Lad about 17 years old, named Issac Allen, a thick chunky Fellow, about five Feet six Inches high, of a pale swarthy Complexion, has dark brown Hair, which he sometimes wears ty'd: Had on and took with him, when he went away, two Tow Shirts, one Check Linnen Ditto, a Pair of short wide Trowsers, a striped Flannel Jacket, a black Ditto, a yellow doubled and twisted Coat, two Hats, a Black Barcelona handkerchief, a Pair of Check Linen Trowsers, two Pair of Stockings, and one Pair of new Shoes. Whoever takes up said Runaway, and brings him to his Master, shall have Two Dollars Reward, and all necessary Charges, paid by me. JOHN FISHER." *Providence Gazette*, Aug. 3, 1771.

3. "SIX DOLLARS Reward. Run away from the Subscriber, last Monday night, an indentured Irish

Servant Lad, named Patrick Sullivan, about 17
Years of Age, smooth faced, has black hair, pretty
tall, and something slim made, has been about
three Months in Country, and can whistle
remarkably soft and fine: Had on, when he went
away, a short blue Sailor's Jacket, a striped under
Ditto, and a Pair of Tow Trowsers. He took with
him a Bundle containing some Shirts and a
brownish coloured half worn Thick-Set Coat.
Whoever takes up said Runaway, and bring him to
my House, on Taunton Green, shall have the above
Reward, and all necessary Charges, paid by,
ROBERT CALDWELL N.B. It is thought he is
gone up the Country. Taunton, November 11,
1771." *Providence Gazette,* November 16, 1771.

4. "Run away from the Subscriber, the Night of the
5th of April last, an Apprentice Lad, named Danile
Bowen, about 20 years of Age, about 5 feet and a
Half high, has brown Hair, grey eyes, is something
round Shouldered, and understands making
Buckles; Had on when he went away a new Felt
Hat, a blue double breasted Jacket, with flowered
Pewter Buttons, striped underflannel Jacket,
Striped Flannel Shirt, Leather Breeches, and Yarn
Stockings. Whoever takes up said Runaway, and
brings him to his Master, Shall have Two Dollars
Reward, and all necessary Charges, paid by
BENJAMIN KINGSLEY. Rehoboth, April 25,
1772." *Providence Gazette*, April 25, 1772.

5. "Ran-away from the Subscriber, living in Gorham,
which joins Falmouth, Cumberland County in the

Massachusetts Province, short Negro Man named
Prince, about 26 Years of Age, 5 Feet some Inches
high, talks broken English, has remarkable small
Ears, and a Jewel Hole in one of them. Had on
almost new Felt Hat, a reddish grey home-made
Cloth Coat Jacket and Breeches, with silk knee
Garters, a dark Callicoe under Jacket, a white
Linnen Shirt, red Collar and Cuffs, to his Coat with
Metal Buttons, white Cotton Stockings, Cald-Skin
Pumps,. It may be he has a Pass. Said Negro plays
tolerable well on a Violin. Whosever will take up
said Negro or bring him to his Master shall have
Sixteen Dollars Reward, and all Charges paid by
WILLIAM M'LEENEN." *Boston Gazette*, June 6,
1774.

6. "RUN away from Moses Cooper of Gloucester, in
the County of Providence, on the 2d of October in
the Evening, a Megro Man named Jack, about 26
Years of Age, of a small Stature, is of the Pawpaw
Tribe, his Teeth filed sharp, has a Scar on the right
side of his Forehead, and is marked up and down
on each side of his Cheeks, and holes in both Ears,
and is blacker than common ; had on when he went
away, a dark kersey Coat, a blue and white striped
Cotton Jacket, a pair of Leather Breeches, and
carried away another pair of Breeches of the same
of the Jacket. Whoever takes up said Fellow and
conveys him to his said Master in Gloucester, or
secures him in any of his Majesty's Goals so that
he may be had again, shall have FIVE DOLLARS
Reward, and all necessary Charges paid by Moses
Cooper. N. B. All Masters of Vessels and others,

are hereby forewarned Secreting or Carrying off said Fellow, as they will answer it at their Peril. Providence, October 7, 1763." *Boston Post Boy*, October 17, 1763.

D. Coats

1. "RUN away from the Subscriber, of Norton, in the County of Bristol, on the 2d Day of December last, an Apprentice lad, named William Haradon, in the 18th Year of his Age, about 5 Feet 10 Inches high; had on when he went away a Felt Hat, a light coloured Surtout, a dark brown homespun Coat, a striped Waistcoat, Leather Breeches, and striped Trowsers. He is of a light Complexion, and has dark brown Hair. If the above Apprentice will return to his Master, his past Misbehaviour will be overlooked. WILLIAM CODINGTON. N.B. All Masters of Vessels and others are cautioned against harbouring, trading with, or carring off said Apprentice, as they would avoid the Penalty of the Law. Norton, March 2, 1773." *Providence Gazette*, March 6, 1773.

2. "DESERTED from Capt. Abimeleck Rigg's Company, in Colonel Talman's Regiment, Benjamin Wood, belonging to Norton, about 5 Feet 9 Inches high, somewhat slim built, of a dark Complexion, has short brown hair; had on when he went away a round Felt Hat, short grey Coat, Jacket and Breeches. Whoever will take up said Deserter, and secure him in any Gaol, or return him to his Company, shall have Five Dollars Reward, and all necessary Charges, paid by ABIMELECK RIGGS, Capt." *Providence Gazette*, Feburary 8, 1777.

3. "RUN away from the subscriber, a Negro lad, named Pero, a smart well built fellow, about 15 years of age, speaks pretty good English, had on a great coat and straight bodied coat, of a brownish grey color, jacket and breeches of a colour somewhat different, home made, greyish stockings, a felt hat almost new, and a fulled cap. Whoever returns said Negro to me, shall have ten dollars reward, and necessary charges. OBADIAH READ. Rehoboth, Dec. 26, 1777." *Providence Gazette*, December 27, 1777.

4. "FOUR DOLLARS REWARD. Ran-away from the Subscriber on the 22d of September, at Night a Negro Man Servant, by the Name of CATO, about Five Feet and Eight Inches high, very thick Lips, speaks broken, and Walks as if he was lame in his Heels. Had on when he went away, a Cloth colour'd Coat, with Pewter Buttons, old Leather Breeches, a Tow Shirt, old Shoes with Silver plate Buckles, wore a Cap, and ?hoves round his Neck, and very high on his Forehead: Carried away with him a Callico Banyan, fine Linen Shirt, Check Linen Trowsers, grey Wigg, also carries or Wears a Felt Hatt with a Silver Lace on it, had a Violin and carries it in a green Bays Bag. Whosoever will return the Runaway to his Master in Winchenden, shall have the above Reward and all necessary Charges, paid by LEVI NICHOL, Winchenden, Sept. 23, 1774." *Boston Gazette*, Monday, October 10, 1774.

E. Waistcoats

1. "RUN away from the Subscriber, of Norton, in the County of Bristol, on the 2d Day of December last, an Apprentice lad, named William Haradon, in the 18th Year of his Age, about 5 Feet 10 Inches high; had on when he went away a Felt Hat, a light coloured Surtout, a dark brown homespun Coat, a striped Waistcoat, Leather Breeches, and striped Trowsers. He is of a light Complexion, and has dark brown Hair. If the above Apprentice will return to his Master, his past Misbehaviour will be overlooked. WILLIAM CODINGTON. N.B. All Masters of Vessels and others are cautioned against harbouring, trading with, or carring off said Apprentice, as they would avoid the Penalty of the Law. Norton, March 2, 1773." *Providence Gazette*, March 6, 1773.

2. "Four Dollars Reward. RANAWAY from his Master MARK HUNKING of Barrington, in New Hampshire, a Negro Servant named CSESAR :--- Had on when he went away, a striped homespun lappel'd Waistcoat, a Tow Shirt, black Serge Breeches, grey Jacket, a pair of Breeches and Jacket of a black and Hemlock dye, striped Tow Trowsers, black and white Yarn Stockings. He is a strait Limb'd Fellow about 5 Feet nine inches high, very white Teeth, smiling Countenance; was bro't up to Farming Work. ---Whoever shall take up said Runaway, and secure him so that his Master may have him again,............MARK HUNKING." *Boston Gazette*, August 1, 1774.

3. "Ran away from his Master on Friday Evening last,
a Negro Boy, named GORREE, about 16 Years of
Age, 5 Feet , 3 Inches High, had on when he went
away, a brown Cloth Coat, dark Velvet Waistcoat,
white Shirt, white Linen Breeches, grey Yarn
Stockings, a pair of Shoes tore at the Heels, with
Pinchback Buckles, an old Felt Hat. Whoever will
take up said Run-away, and secure him, and give
Information to the Subscriber, for that he may have
him again, shall have a handsome Reward and
necessary Charges paid by DANIEL VOSE.
Milton." *Boston Gazette,* May 30, 1774.

F. Breeches

1. "Run away from the Subscriber, the Night of the
5th of April last, an Apprentice Lad, named Danile
Bowen, about 20 years of Age, about 5 feet and a
Half high, has brown Hair, grey eyes, is something
round Shouldered, and understands making
Buckles; Had on when he went away a new Felt
Hat, a blue double breasted Jacket, with flowered
Pewter Buttons, striped underflannel Jacket,
Striped Flannel Shirt, Leather Breeches, and Yarn
Stockings. Whoever takes up said Runaway, and
brings him to his Master, Shall have Two Dollars
Reward, and all necessary Charges, paid by
BENJAMIN KINGSLEY. Rehoboth, April 25,
1772." *Providence Gazette*, April 25, 1772.

2. "RUN away from the Subscriber, of Norton, in the
County of Bristol, on the 2d Day of December last,
an Apprentice lad, named William Haradon, in the
18th Year of his Age, about 5 Feet 10 Inches high;

had on when he went away a Felt Hat, a light coloured Surtout, a dark brown homespun Coat, a striped Waistcoat, Leather Breeches, and striped Trowsers. He is of a light Complexion, and has dark brown Hair. If the above Apprentice will return to his Master, his past Misbehaviour will be overlooked. WILLIAM CODINGTON. N.B. All Masters of Vessels and others are cautioned against harbouring, trading with, or carring off said Apprentice, as they would avoid the Penalty of the Law. Norton, March 2, 1773." *Providence Gazette*, March 6, 1773.

3. "DESERTED on the 13th Inst. from Ensign Springer's Company, commanded by Col. Sayles, a private Soldier named Wilham Middleton, says he was born in Ireland; he is of a light Complexion, pitted with the Small-pox; had on when he went away a short light coloured Sailor's Jacket, Leather Breeches, and white woolen Hose. Whoever takes up said Deserter, so that he may be returned to his Regiment or Company, shall receive Five Dollars Reward and all reasonable Charges, paid by me, JOSEPH SPRINGER, Ensign." *Providence Gazette*, December 21, 1776.

4. "For Sale by, Humphrey Palmer, At his shop in Rehoboth, Blue broadcloth, scarlet and green baise, deerskin breeches, loaf and brown sugar, choice West India Rum, molasses, Lisbon salt, pepper, alspice, indigo, copperas, allum, pins, needles, gunpowder, shot, writing paper, codfish, Woman's thimbles, ivory and horn combs, sleeve buttons, and sundry other articles: for some of which the emmissions of Continental money of May 1777,

and April 1778, will not be refused, for some of the above goods also wood, grain, butter, cheese, flax, and other produce will be taken in pay, and the articles sold on lower terms than they lately have been." *Providence Gazette,* Feburary 20, 1779.

5. "Ten Dollar Reward. RAN AWAY from the Subscriber, Joseph Moors, of Groton, in the County of Middlesex, and Province of Massachusetts-Bay, a Malatto Man Servant, names TITUS, sbout 20 Years of Age, of a middling Statue, wears, short curl'd Hair, has one of his Fore Teeth broke out, took with his a blue Surdan, a Snuff coulor'd Coat, and a Pair, of white wash'd Leather Breeches, a Pair of new Cow-hide Pumps, and a Fur'd Hat with large Brims, and sundry other Articles of Wearing Apparel.---Whoever will take of said Servant and confine him in any of his Majesty's Goals ....Joseph Moors." *Boston Gazette,* July 25, 1774.

6. "Four Dollars Reward. RANAWAY from his Master MARK HUNKING of Barrington, in New Hampshire, a Negro Servant named CSESAR :--- Had on when he went away, a striped homespun lappel'd Waistcoat, a Tow Shirt, black Serge Breeches, grey Jacket, a pair of Breeches and Jacket of a black and Hemlock dye, striped Tow Trowsers, black and white Yarn Stockings. He is a strait Limb'd Fellow about 5 Feet nine inches high, very white Teeth, smiling Countenance; was bro't up to Farming Work. ---Whoever shall take up said Runaway, and secure him so that his Master may

have him again,.............MARK HUNKING."
Boston Gazette, August 1, 1774.

7. "Stop Thief and Runaway Man Servant. Whereas
William Hayward, Baker, absconded himself from
my Service 16th March, 1774, and took with him to
the Value of eight pounds , L. M. and be being
taken and convicted, voluntarily Bound himself, to
serve me Six Months, to Pay Damages & Cost: and
he last Night absconded himself again; had on an
old Felt Hat, an old cloth colour'd Coat and
Waistcoat, check'd Woolen Shirt, a Pair of new
cloth colour'd Breeches, a Pair of old pale blue
Stockings, and a Pair of single Sole Shoes.--Said
Hayward is about Thirty-three Years of Age, Five
Feet Five Inches high, darkish, short Hair, and
down look like a Rogue and Thief.----Whossoever
will take up said Servant and Notify me the
Subscriber so that I may have him again, shall have
FIVE DOLLARS reward. Paid by me, ISAAC
SHERMAN, Marlboro April 9, 1774. All Bakers
are hereby cautioned against Employing said
Servant." *Boston Gazette*, May 9, 1774.

8. Run-away from the Subscriber, living in Gorham,
which joins Falmouth, Cumberland County in the
Massachusetts Province, short Negro Man named
Prince, about 26 Years of Age, 5 Feet some Inches
high, talks broken English, has remarkable small
Ears, and a Jewel Hole in one of them. Had on
almost new Felt Hat, a reddish grey home-made
Cloth Coat Jacket and Breeches, with silk knee
Garters, a dark Callicoe under Jacket, a white

Linnen Shirt, red Collar and Cuffs, to his Coat with
Metal Buttons, white Cotton Stockings, Cald-Skin
Pumps,. It may be he has a Pass. Said Negro plays
tolerable well on a Violin. Whosever will take up
said Negro or bring him to his Master shall have
Sixteen Dollars Reward, and all Charges paid by
WILLIAM M'LEENEN." *Boston Gazette*, June 6,
1774.

9. "Rehoboth, August 12, 1763, Runaway from his
master, Samuel Whitman, of Rehoboth, on Monday
the 25th of July, an Apprentice Lad, about 17 years
of age, named Edward Green, a Shoemaker by
trade. Had on when he went away, a blue coat,
green Jacket, a light coloured pair of breeches, and
wore his own hair: He is a short, thick fellow.
Whoever takes up said lad, and returns him to his
Master, or secures him in any of his Majesty's
Gaols, so that he may be had again, shall receive
THREE DOLLARS Reward, and all necessary
Charges paid, by, SAMUEL WHITMANN.B. All
Masters of Vessels and others are forewarned
either secreting or carring off said Fellow, as they
would avoid the Penalty of the Law." *Providence
Gazette*, August 13, 1763.

G. Trousers

1. "Ran away from me the Subscriber, on the 4th
instant, an apprentice Lad named Uriah Stone,
about 18 years of Age; he is Short in Stature, and
of a dark Complexion. He had on when he went
away a Flannel Jacket without Sleeves, a striped
Tow Shirt, a Pair of Short Wide Trowsers, and an

Old Felt Hat. Whoever Apprehends said Lad and brings him to his Master Sall be resonably rewarded for their Trouble. NATHANIEL BROWN Rehoboth, August 13, 1767." *Providence Gazette,* August 15, 1767.

2. "Ran-away from the Subscriber in Dartmouth, on the 20th of this Instant, a Molatto Fellow named Gideon Halley or Gideon Cheat, about 5 Feet and six Inches high, about 30 Years old, a thick built Fellow, wears long Hair tied up; had on when he went away , a brown Kersey Flannel Jacket, strip'd Flannel Shirt, strip'd Flannel Trowsers, and a Beaver Hat much worn, looks much like an Indian, brags much of his being in the Army Westward the last War. Whosoever will secure him in any of his Majesty's Goals or deliver him to his Master shall have FOUR DOLLARS Reward and all necessary Charges paid by JOSEPH RUSSEL. Dartmouth, June 24, 1768." *Boston News Letter,* July 14, 1768.

3. "SIX DOLLARS Reward Run away from the Subscriber, last Monday night, an indentured Irish Servant Lad, named Patrick Sullivan, about 17 Years of Age, smooth faced, has black hair, pretty tall, and something slim made, has been about three Months in Country, and can whistle remarkably soft and fine: Had on, when he went away, a short blue Sailor's Jacket, a striped under Ditto, and a Pair of Tow Trowsers. He took with him a Bundle containing some Shirts and a brownish coloured half worn Thick-Set Coat.

Whoever takes up said Runaway, and bring him to
my House, on Taunton Green, shall have the above
Reward, and all necessary Charges, paid by,
ROBERT CALDWELL N.B. It is thought he is
gone up the Country. Taunton, November 11,
1771." *Providence Gazette*, November 16, 1771.

4. "RUN away from the Subscriber, of Norton, in the
    County of Bristol, on the 2d Day of December last,
    an Apprentice lad, named William Haradon, in the
    18th Year of his Age, about 5 Feet 10 Inches high;
    had on when he went away a Felt Hat, a light
    coloured Surtout, a dark brown homespun Coat, a
    striped Waistcoat, Leather Breeches, and striped
    Trowsers. He is of a light Complexion, and has
    dark brown Hair. If the above Apprentice will
    return to his Master, his past Misbehaviour will be
    overlooked. WILLIAM CODINGTON. N.B. All
    Masters of Vessels and others are cautioned against
    harbouring, trading with, or carring off said
    Apprentice, as they would avoid the Penalty of the
    Law. Norton, March 2, 1773." *Providence
    Gazette*, March 6, 1773.

5. "Four Dollars Reward. RANAWAY from his
    Master MARK HUNKING of Barrington, in New
    Hampshire, a Negro Servant named CSESAR :---
    Had on when he went away, a striped homespun
    lappel'd Waistcoat, a Tow Shirt, black Serge
    Breeches, grey Jacket, a pair of Breeches and
    Jacket of a black and Hemlock dye, striped Tow
    Trowsers, black and white Yarn Stockings. He is a
    strait Limb'd Fellow about 5 Feet nine inches high,
    very white Teeth, smiling Countenance; was bro't
    up to Farming Work. ---Whoever shall take up said
    Runaway, and secure him so that his Master may

have him again,............MARK HUNKING."
Boston Gazette, August 1, 1774.

6. "FOUR DOLLARS REWARD. Ran-away from
the Subscriber on the 22d of September, at Night a
Negro Man Servant, by the Name of CATO, about
Five Feet and Eight Inches high, very thick Lips,
speaks broken, and Walks as if he was lame in his
Heels. Had on when he went away, a Cloth
colour'd Coat, with Pewter Buttons, old Leather
Breeches, a Tow Shirt, old Shoes with Silver plate
Buckles, wore a Cap, and ?hoves round his Neck,
and very high on his Forehead: Carried away with
him a Callico Banyan, fine Linen Shirt, Check
Linen Trowsers, grey Wigg, also carries or Wears a
Felt Hatt with a Silver Lace on it, had a Violin and
carries it in a green Bays Bag. Whosoever will
return the Runaway to his Master in Winchenden,
shall have the above Reward and all necessary
Charges, paid by LEVI NICHOL, Winchenden,
Sept. 23, 1774." *Boston Gazette*, Monday, October
10, 1774.

H. Stockings

1. "Run away from the Subscriber, the Night of the
5th of April last, an Apprentice Lad, named Danile
Bowen, about 20 years of Age, about 5 feet and a
Half high, has brown Hair, grey eyes, is something
round Shouldered, and understands making
Buckles; Had on when he went away a new Felt
Hat, a blue double breasted Jacket, with flowered
Pewter Buttons, striped underflannel Jacket,
Striped Flannel Shirt, Leather Breeches, and Yarn

Stockings. Whoever takes up said Runaway, and brings him to his Master, Shall have Two Dollars Reward, and all necessary Charges, paid by BENJAMIN KINGSLEY. Rehoboth, April 25, 1772." *Providence Gazette*, April 25, 1772.

2. "DESERTED on the 13th Inst. from Ensign Springer's Company, commanded by Col. Sayles, a private Soldier named Wilham Middleton, says he was born in Ireland; he is of a light Complexion, pitted with the Small-pox; had on when he went away a short light coloured Sailor's Jacket, Leather Breeches, and white woolen Hose. Whoever takes up said Deserter, so that he may be returned to his Regiment or Company, shall receive Five Dollars Reward and all reasonable Charges, paid by me, JOSEPH SPRINGER, Ensign." *Providence Gazette*, December 21, 1776.

3. "RUN away from the subscriber, a Negro lad, named Pero, a smart well built fellow, about 15 years of age, speaks pretty good English, had on a great coat and straight bodied coat, of a brownish grey color, jacket and breeches of a colour somewhat different, home made, greyish stockings, a felt hat almost new, and a fulled cap. Whoever returns said Negro to me, shall have ten dollars reward, and necessary charges. OBADIAH READ. Rehoboth, Dec. 26, 1777." *Providence Gazette*, December 27, 1777.

4. "Ran-away from the Subscriber, living in Gorham, which joins Falmouth, Cumberland County in the Massachusetts Province, short Negro Man named

Prince, about 26 Years of Age, 5 Feet some Inches high, talks broken English, has remarkable small Ears, and a Jewel Hole in one of them. Had on almost new Felt Hat, a reddish grey home-made Cloth Coat Jacket and Breeches, with silk knee Garters, a dark Callicoe under Jacket, a white Linnen Shirt, red Collar and Cuffs, to his Coat with Metal Buttons, white Cotton Stockings, Cald-Skin Pumps,. It may be he has a Pass. Said Negro plays tolerable well on a Violin. Whosever will take up said Negro or bring him to his Master shall have Sixteen Dollars Reward, and all Charges paid by WILLIAM M'LEENEN." *Boston Gazette*, June 6, 1774.

5. "Four Dollars Reward. RANAWAY from his Master MARK HUNKING of Barrington, in New Hampshire, a Negro Servant named CSESAR :--- Had on when he went away, a striped homespun lappel'd Waistcoat, a Tow Shirt, black Serge Breeches, grey Jacket, a pair of Breeches and Jacket of a black and Hemlock dye, striped Tow Trowsers, black and white Yarn Stockings. He is a strait Limb'd Fellow about 5 Feet nine inches high, very white Teeth, smiling Countenance; was bro't up to Farming Work. ---Whoever shall take up said Runaway, and secure him so that his Master may have him again,............MARK HUNKING." *Boston Gazette*, August 1, 1774.

6. "Stop Thief and Runaway Man Servant. Whereas William Hayward, Baker, absconded himself from my Service 16th March, 1774, and took with him to

the Value of eight pounds , L. M. and be being
taken and convicted, voluntarily Bound himself, to
serve me Six Months, to Pay Damages & Cost: and
he last Night absconded himself again; had on an
old Felt Hat, an old cloth colour'd Coat and
Waistcoat, check'd Woolen Shirt, a Pair of new
cloth colour'd Breeches, a Pair of old pale blue
Stockings, and a Pair of single Sole Shoes.--Said
Hayward is about Thirty-three Years of Age, Five
Feet Five Inches high, darkish, short Hair, and
down look like a Rogue and Thief.----Whossoever
will take up said Servant and Notify me the
Subscriber so that I may have him again, shall have
FIVE DOLLARS reward. Paid by me, ISAAC
SHERMAN, Marlboro April 9, 1774. All Bakers
are hereby cautioned against Employing said
Servant." *Boston Gazette*, May 9, 1774.

7.   "Joseph Peirce, At his Shop the North Side of the
     Town House, Boston, -Informs his Customers,
     and   Others, that he has imported from LONDON
     per Capt. Scott,
     A fresh Assortment of Goods, Which he will sell at
     very reasonable Profits, for ready money. Amongst
     his Goods are some Men's exceeding neat 3 and 4
     thread, plain and Patent Rib worsted Hose of
     various Colours,-some remarkable cheap scarlet
     Broadcloth, Beaver Coatings, Lambskins, Kerseys,
     Baizes, scarlet Whitney-Cordusoy, Royal Rib,
     Crimson Cape Velvet, Patens, best English made
     Shoes, and Pumps, Clogs, and Goloshoes, Muffs,
     Patent Cake Blacking, and Cake Ink, Men's white,
     and colour'd patent Rib, and plain Silk Hose, plain

black ditto, -Boys black Hatts.- A few *elegant
enameled India China Punch-Bowls*, blue & white
India half pints Bowls, ditto and Saucers,
Breakfast, and Tea Cups and Saucers, blue and
white Octagon Plates.- *True Sable Muffs, and
Tippets,*-together with more Articles than is
convenient to enumerate in an Advertisement."
Boston Gazette, January 3, 1774.

8. "10 DOLLARS REWARD Ran away from his
Master Jonathan Norwood, of Gloucester, (Cape-
Ann) on the 22d of September Inst. a very likely
Negro Man named Newport, about 5 Feet and half
high, a strait limb Fellow, about 35 Years of Age,
very likely in the Face ; had on when he Ran away
a good Castor Hat, clean white Frock, a woolen
Shirt, white short Trousers, white ribb'd worsted
Stockings, pretty good Pumps, very large Silver
Buckels in his Shoes, plays well on a Violin, and is
a very active Fellow, and as he has Money with
him, 'tis likely he will change his Dress, as he took
other Cloaths with him. Whoever apprehends the
said Negro, and will bring him to his said Master,
or secure him, shall have Ten Dollars Reward, and
all necessary Charges paid by Jonathan Norwood."
Boston Post Boy, October 1, 1764.

I. No Stockings

1. Ran-away from his Master, Jabez Hatch, of
Boston, on the 25th Inst. a Negro Man named
Caesar, a stout well set Fellow, speaks good
English: had on when he went away, a Froost and
Trowsers, check Shirt, no Stockings, an old pair

Shoes. Whoever will bring said Negro to his
Master, or secure him so that he may have him
shall have TWO DOLLARS Reward, and all
necessary Charges paid. Jabez Hatch." *Boston
News Letter*, August 4, 1768.

J. Shoes and Footwear

1. "In the Night of the 21st Instant the Shop of the
   subscriber was broke open and robbed of the
   following Articles, viz., 10 pair Calfskin shoes, one
   Pair of Calfskin Boots, with stiff Tops, between 50
   and 60 pounds of Flax, and 16 Dozen of Horn
   Buttons. Whoever will secure the Theif, with the
   Goods, shall have fifty Dollars Reward, or for the
   Goods only Thirty Dollars, and necessary Charges.
   paid by the subscriber, at Capt. Daniel Hunts in
   Rehoboth. JOSEPH WHEATON HUNT.
   Rehoboth, Aug. 24, 1778." *Providence Gazette*,
   August 29, 1778, September 5, 1778, and
   September 12, 1778.

2. "Ten Dollar Reward. RAN AWAY from the
   Subscriber, Joseph Moors, of Groton, in the
   County of Middlesex, and Province of
   Massachusetts-Bay, a Malatto Man Servant, names
   TITUS, sbout 20 Years of Age, of a middling
   Statue, wears, short curl'd Hair, has one of his Fore
   Teeth broke out, took with his a blue Surdan, a
   Snuff coulor'd Coat, and a Pair, of white wash'd
   Leather Breeches, a Pair of new Cow-hide Pumps,
   and a Fur'd Hat with large Brims, and sundry other
   Articles of Wearing Apparel.---Whoever will take
   of said Servant and confine him in any of his

Majesty's Goals ....Joseph Moors." *Boston Gazette,* July 25, 1774.

3. "FOUR DOLLARS REWARD. Ran-away from the Subscriber on the 22d of September, at Night a Negro Man Servant, by the Name of CATO, about Five Feet and Eight Inches high, very thick Lips, speaks broken, and Walks as if he was lame in his Heels. Had on when he went away, a Cloth colour'd Coat, with Pewter Buttons, old Leather Breeches, a Tow Shirt, old Shoes with Silver plate Buckles, wore a Cap, and ?hoves round his Neck, and very high on his Forehead: Carried away with him a Callico Banyan, fine Linen Shirt, Check Linen Trowsers, grey Wigg, also carries or Wears a Felt Hatt with a Silver Lace on it, had a Violin and carries it in a green Bays Bag. Whosoever will return the Runaway to his Master in Winchenden, shall have the above Reward and all necessary Charges, paid by LEVI NICHOL, Winchenden, Sept. 23, 1774." *Boston Gazette*, Monday, October 10, 1774.

4. "Stop Thief and Runaway Man Servant. Whereas William Hayward, Baker, absconded himself from my Service 16th March, 1774, and took with him to the Value of eight pounds , L. M. and be being taken and convicted, voluntarily Bound himself, to serve me Six Months, to Pay Damages & Cost: and he last Night absconded himself again; had on an old Felt Hat, an old cloth colour'd Coat and Waistcoat, check'd Woolen Shirt, a Pair of new cloth colour'd Breeches, a Pair of old pale blue

Stockings, and a Pair of single Sole Shoes.--Said
Hayward is about Thirty-three Years of Age, Five
Feet Five Inches high, darkish, short Hair, and
down look like a Rogue and Thief.----Whossoever
will take up said Servant and Notify me the
Subscriber so that I may have him again, shall have
FIVE DOLLARS reward. Paid by me, ISAAC
SHERMAN, Marlboro April 9, 1774. All Bakers
are hereby cautioned against Employing said
Servant." *Boston Gazette*, May 9, 1774.

5. "Ran away from his Mistress Isabel Caldwell, of
    Rutland District, in the County of Worchester, the
    25th of May last, a Negro Man about 30 Years of
    Age, named Mingo, speaks middling good English,
    a sprightly little Fellow, about five Feet and five or
    six Inches high : Had on when he went away, an all
    wool brown colour'd great Coat with large white
    metal Buttons, and an all wool Jacket of the same
    Colour ; a blue and white striped woolen Shirt, and
    a worsted Cap, an old Hat, A Pair of leather
    Breeches, and light blue Stockings ; a Pair of Shoes
    about half worn, tied with leather Strings." *Boston
    News Letter*, August 13, 1765.

K. Buttons

1. "In the Night of the 21st Instant the Shop of the
    subscriber was broke open and robbed of the
    following Articles, viz., 10 pair Calfskin shoes, one
    Pair of Calfskin Boots, with stiff Tops, between 50
    and 60 pounds of Flax, and 16 Dozen of Horn
    Buttons. Whoever will secure the Theif, with the
    Goods, shall have fifty Dollars Reward, or for the

Goods only Thirty Dollars, and necessary Charges.
paid by the subscriber, at Capt. Daniel Hunts in
Rehoboth. JOSEPH WHEATON HUNT.
Rehoboth, Aug. 24, 1778." *Providence Gazette*,
August 29, 1778, September 5, 1778, and
September 12, 1778.

APPENDIX J

EXCERPTS FROM THE LETTERS OF JOSEPH WARREN TO THE CONTINENTAL CONGRESS: THE BATTLE OF LEXINGTON

In Provincial Congress, Watertown, April 26, 1775.

Sir,

From the entire Confidence we Repose in your faithfulness and Abilities, we consider it the happiness of this Colony, that the important trust of Agency for it, in this day of unequalled Distress, is devolved on your hands, and we doubt not, your Attachment to the Cause and liberties of Mankind, will make every possible Exertion in our behalf, a Pleasure to you; altho' our circumstances will compell us often to Interrupt your repose, by Matters that will surely give you Pain. A singular instance hereof is the Occasion of the present letter. The Contents of this Packet, will be our Apology for Troubling you with it.

From these, you will see, how and by whom we are at last Plunged into the horrors of a most unnatural war. Our enemies, we are told, have despatched to G[reat] Britain a fallacious Account of the Tragedy they have begun; to prevent the operation of which, to the Publick injury, we have engaged the Vessel that conveys this to you, as a Packet in the service of this Colony, and we Request your Assistance in supplying Captain Derby, who commands her, with such Necessaries as he shall want, on the Credit of your Constituents in Massachusetts Bay.

But we most ardently wish, that the several papers herewith Inclosed, may be immediately printed, and Disperced thro' every Town in England, and especially communicated to the

Lord Mayor, Aldermen, and Common Council of the city of London, that they may take such Order thereon, as they may think Proper. And we are Confident your fidelity will make such improvement of them, as shall convince all, who are not determined to be in everlasting blandness, that it is the united efforts of both Englands, that must save either. But that whatever Price our Brethren in the one, may he pleased to put on their constitutional liberties, we are authorized to assure you, that the inhabitants of the other, with the Greatest Unanimity, are inflexibly resolved to sell theirs only at the Price of their lives.

Sign'd by order of the Provincial Congress,
Joseph Warren, President, P. T.

A true Copy from the original Minutes,
Samuel Freeman, Secretary, P. T.

The depositions relative to the commencement of hostilities, are as follows[363]:

---

[363] On April 22d. The Massachusetts Congress appointed a committee to collect testimony on the conduct of the British troops in their route to Concord, to be sent to England by the first ship from Salem. Mr. Gerry, Colonel Cushing, Colonel Barrett, Captain Stone, Dr. Taylor, Messrs. Sullivan, Freeman and Watson, and Esquire Jonas Dix constituted this committee; and on the 23d, Gerry and Cushing were joined with Dr. Church to draw up an account of the "massacre" of the 19th. The report and narrative were submitted on the 26th, and a number of scribes named to make duplicate copies. One set was entrusted to Captain Richard Derby, who was to hasten to London and deliver them to Franklin. On May 2d, Gerry, Warren, Dexter, Col. Warren and Garish were ordered to send a second set to the Southern colonies, to be transmitted to London, and a third set to the Continental Congress. The copies sent to the Congress are in Papers of the Continental Congress, No. 65, vol. I, folios 11--51. These depositions were printed in the following pamphlet:
A Narrative, of the Excursion and Ravages of the King's Troops Under the Command of General Gage, On the nineteenth of April, 1775. Together with the Depositions Taken by Order of Congress, To support the Truth of it. Published by Authority. Massachusetts-Bay: Worcester, Printed by Isaiah Thomas, by order of the Provincial Congress. Copies are in the

No. 1 Lexington, April 25, 1775.

We, Solomon Brown, Jonathan Loring, and Elijah Sanderson, all of lawful Age, and of Lexington, in the County of Middlesex, and Collony of the Massachusett Bay, in New England, do testifie and declare, that on the evening of the Eighteenth of April, Instant, being on the Road between Concord and Lexington, and all of us mounted on Horses, we were, about ten of the Clock, suddenly surprized by nine Persons, whom we took to be Regular Officers, who Rode up to us, mounted and armed, each having a Pistol in His Hand, and after Putting Pistols to our Breasts, and seizing the Bridles of our Horses, they swore, that if we stirred another step, we should be all Dead Men, upon which we surrendered our selves. They Detained us until Two o'Clock the next morning, in which time they searched and greatly abused us; having first enquired about the Magazine at Concord, whether any Guards were posted there, and whether the bridges were up, and said four or five Regiments of Regulars would be in Possession of the stores soon; they then brought us back to Lexington, eat the Horses Bridles and Girts, turned them Loose, and then Left us.

Solomon Brown,
Jonathan Loring,
Elijah Sanderson.

Middlesex, ff. April 25, 1775.

Jonn Loring, Solomon Brown, and Elijah Sanderson, being duly cautioned to Testify the whole Truth, made solemn Oath to the Truth of the above Deposition by them subscribed.

Coram

       Just. Pacis[364].

American Antiquarian Society.
[364] Each deposition is sworn to before justices of the peace, and duly attested before Nathaniel Gorham, notary and Tabellion public.

William Reed

Josiah Johnson

William Stickney

Lexington, April 25, 1775.

I, Elijah Saunderson, above named, do further testifie and declare, that I was on Lexington Common, the Morning of the Nineteenth of April, aforesaid, having been dismissed by the Officers abovementioned, and saw a Large Body of Regular Troops advancing toward Lexington Company, many of whom were then dispersing. I heard one of the Regulars, whom I took to be an officer, say, "Damn them, we will have them," and immediately the Regulars shouted aloud, Run and fired upon the Lexington Company, which did not fire a Gun before the Regulars Discharged on them; Eight of the Lexington Company were killed while they were dispersing, and at a Considerable Distance from each other, and Many wounded, and altho' a spectator, I narrowly Escaped with my Life.

Elijah Saunderson.

Middlesex, ff. April 25, 1775.

Elijah Saunderson, above named, being Duly Cautioned to Testify the whole Truth, made Solemn Oath to the Truth of the above Deposition by him subscribed.

Coram.

William Reed

Josiah Johnson

William Stickney

Just. Pacis.

No. 2 Lexington, April 23, 1775.

I, Thomas Rice Willard, of lawful age, do Testify and Declare, that being in the House of Daniel Harrington, of said Lexington, on the Nineteenth Instant, in the morning, about half an hour before sunrise, [I] looked out at the window of said house, and saw (as I suppose) about four hundred Regulars in one Body, coming up the road, and marched toward the north part of the Common, back of the meeting-house of said Lexington; and as soon as said Regulars were against the east end of the meeting-house, the Commanding Officer said something, what I know not; but upon that the Regulars ran till they came within about eight or nine rods of about an Hundred of the Militia of Lexington, who were collected on said Common, at which time the Militia of Lexington dispersed; then the Officers made an huzza, and the private Soldiers succeeded them: Directly after this, an officer rode before the Regulars to the other side of the body, and hallooed after the Militia of said Lexington, and said, "Lay Down your Arms, Damn you, why Don't you lay Down your arms?" and that there was not a Gun fired till the Militia of Lexington were Dispersed; and further saith not.

Thomas Rice Willard.[365]

No. 3 Lexington, April 25, 1775.

Simon Winship, of Lexington, in the County of Middlesex,

---

[365] Sworn to before William Reed, Jonathan Hastings and Duncan Ingraham.

and province of Massachusetts Bay, New England, being of lawful age, testifieth and saith, that on the Nineteenth of April Instant, about four o'Clock in the Morning, as he was passing the Publick Road in said Lexington, peaceably and unarmed, about two miles and an half distant from the meeting-House in said Lexington, he was met by a Body of the Kings regular Troops, and being stop'd by some Officers of said Troops, was Commanded to Dismount; upon asking why he must dismount, he was obliged by force to Quit his Horse, and ordered to march in the midst of the Body, and being Examined whether he had been Warning the Minute Men, he answered No, but had been out, and was then returning to his fathers. Said Winship further testifies, that he marched with said Troops, untill he came within about half-a-Quarter of a Mile of said meeting-House, where an Officer commanded the Troops to halt, and then to prime and load: this being done, the said Troops marched on till they came within a few Rods of Captain Parkers Company, who were partly collected on the place of parade, when said Winship observed an Officer at the head of said Troops, flourishing his Sword, and with a Loud Voice, giving the word fire, fire, which was instantly followed by a Discharge of Arms from said regular Troops, and said Winship is positive, and in the most solemn manner declares, that there was no Discharge of arms on either side, till the word fire was given, by the said Officer as above.

Simon Winship.[366]

No. 4 Lexington, April 25, 1775.

I, John Parker, of lawful Age, and Commander of the Militia

---

[366] Sworn to before William Reed and Josiah Johnson.

in Lexington, do testify and declare, that on the 19th Instant in the Morning, about one of the Clock, being informed that there were a Number of Regular Officers, riding up and down the Road, stopping and insulting People as they passed the Road; and also was informed that a Number of Regular Troops were on their March from Boston in order to take the Province Stores at Concord, ordered our Militia to meet on the Common in said Lexington to consult what to do, and concluded not to be discovered, nor meddle or make with said Regular Troops (if they should approach) unless they should insult or molest us; and, upon their sudden Approach, I immediately ordered our Militia to disperse, and not to fire:-- Immediately said Troops made their appearance and rushed furiously, fired upon, and killed eight of our Party without receiving any Provocation therefor from us.

John Parker.[367]

No. 5 Lexington, April 24, 1775.

I, John Robins, being of lawful Age, do Testifye and say, that

---

[367] Sworn to before William Reed, Josiah Johnson, and William Stickney.

on the Nineteenth Instant, the Company under the Command
of Captain John Parker, being drawn up (sometime before sun
Rise) on the Green or Common, and I being in the front Rank,
there suddenly appear'd a Number of the Kings Troops, about
a Thousand, as I thought, at the distance of about 60 or 70
yards from us Huzzaing, and on a quick pace towards us, with
three Officers in their front on Horse Back, and on full Gallop
towards us, the foremost of which cryed, throw down your
Arms ye Villains, ye Rebels! upon which said Company
Dispersing, the foremost of the three Officers order'd their
Men, saying, fire, by God, fire! at which Moment we received
a very heavy and close fire from them, at which Instant, being
wounded, I fell, and several of our men were shot Dead by me.
Captain Parker's men I believe had not then fired a Gun, and
further the Deponent saith not.

John Robins.

No. 6 Lexington, April 25, 1775.

We, Benjamin Tidd, of Lexington, and Joseph Abbot, of
Lincoln, in the County of Middlesex, and Colony of
Massachusetts Bay, in New England, of lawful age, do testify
and Declare that, on the morning of the Nineteenth of April
Instant, about 5 o'Clock, being on Lexington Common, and
mounted on Horses, we saw a Body of regular Troops
Marching up to the Lexington Company, which was then
dispersing: Soon after, the regulars fired, first, a few guns,
which we took to be pistols from some of the Regulars who
were mounted on Horses, and then the said Regulars fired a
Volley or two before any guns were fired by the Lexington
Company; our Horses immediately started, and we rode off.
And further say not.

Benjamin Tidd,
Joseph Abbot.[368]

No. 7 Lexington, April 25, 1775.

---

[368] Sworn to before William Reed, Josiah Johnson and William Stickney.

We, Nathaniel Mulliken, Phillip Russell, Moses Harrington,
jun. Thomas and Daniel Harrington, William Grimes, William
Tidd, Isaac Hastings, Jonas Stone, jun. James Wyman,
Thaddeus Harrington, John Chandler, Joshua Reed, jun.
Joseph Simonds, Phineas Smith, John Chandler, jun. Reuben
Lock, Joel Viles, Nathan Reed, Samuel Tidd, Benjamin Lock,
Thomas Winship, Simeon Snow, John Smith, Moses
Harrington the 3d, Joshua Reed, Ebenezer Parker, John
Harrington, Enoch Wellington, John Hosmer, Isaac Green,
Phineas Stearns, Isaac Durant, and Thomas Headley, jun. all
of Lawful age, and Inhabitants of Lexington in the County of
Middlesex, and Colony of the Massachusetts Bay, in New
England, do testify and declare, that on the 19th of April
instant, about one or two o'Clock in the morning, being
Informed that several officers of the Regulars had, the evening
before, been riding up and down the Road, and had detained
and Insulted the Inhabitants passing the same; and also
understanding that a body of Regulars were marching from
Boston towards Concord, with intent (as it was supposed) to
take the Stores, belonging to the Colony, in that town, we
were alarmed, and having met at the place of our Company's
Parade, were dismissed by our Captain, John Parker, for the
Present, with orders to be ready to attend at the beat of the
drum. We further testify and declare, that about five o'Clock in
the morning, hearing our drum beat, we proceeded towards the
Parade, and soon found that a Large body of troops were
marching towards us: Some of our Company were coming up
to the Parade, and others had reached it; at which time the
Company began to disperse: Whilst our backs were Turned on
the Troops, we were fired on by them, and a number of our
men were Instantly killed and wounded. Not a Gun was fired,
by any Person in our Company, on the Regulars, to our
knowledge, before they fired on us, and they continued Firing
untill we had all made our Escape.

No. 8 Lexington, April 25, 1775.

We, Nathanael Parkhurst, Jonas Parker, John Munroe, jun. John Winship, Solomon Pierce, John Muzzy, Abner Meeds, John Bridge, jun. Ebenezer Bowman, William Munroe the 3d, Micah Hager, Samuel Saunderson, Samuel Hastings, and James Brown, of Lexington, in the County of Middlesex, and Colony of the Massachusetts Bay, in New England, and all of Lawfull age, do Testify and Say, that, on the Morning of the Nineteenth of April Instant, about one or two o'Clock, being informed, that a Number of Regular Officers had been Riding up and down the Road the evening and night preceding, and that some of the Inhabitants, as they were passing, had been Insulted by the Officers, and stopped by them; and being also Informed, that the Regular Troops were on their March from Boston, in order (as it was said) to take the Colony Stores, then Deposited at Concord, we met on the Parade of our Company in this town; After the Company had Collected, we were Ordered, by Captain Parker, (who Commanded us) to Disperse for the Present, and to be Ready to attend the beat of the Drum, and Accordingly the Company went into houses near the place of Parade. We further Testify and Say, that, about five o'Clock in the morning, we attended the beat of our Drum, and were formed on the Parade; we were faced towards the Regulars then marching up to us, and some of our Company were comeing to the parade with their backs towards the Troops, and Others on the parade, began to Disperse when the Regulars fired on the Company, before a Gun was fired by any of our company on them. They killed eight of our company, and wounded several, and continued their fire, until we had all made our escape.

[Signed by each of the deponents.]

No. 9 Lexington, April 25, 1775.

I, Timothy Smith, of Lexington, in the County of Middlesex, and Colony of Massachusetts bay, in New England, being of lawful age, do testify and declare, that, on the morning of the nineteenth of April instant, being at Lexington Common, as a spectator, I saw a large body of regular troops marching up towards the Lexington company, then dispersing, and likewise saw the regular troops fire on the Lexington company, before the latter fired a gun; I immediately ran, and a volley was discharged at me, which put me in imminent danger of losing my life; I soon returned to the Common, and saw eight of the Lexington men who were killed, and lay bleeding at a considerable distance from each other; and several were wounded: And further saith not.

Timothy Smith.[369]

No. 10.Lexington, April 25, 1775.

---

[369] Sworn to before William Reed, Josiah Johnson and William Stickney.

We, Levi Mead and Levi Harrington, both of Lexington, in the County of Middlesex, and Colony of the Massachusetts bay, in New England, and of lawfull age, do Testify and Declare, that on the morning of the Nineteenth of April, being on Lexington Common, as spectators, we saw a Large body of Regular Troops marching up towards the Lexington Company, and some of the Regulars, on Horses, whom we took to be officers, Fired a Pistol or two on the Lexington Company, which were then dispersing: These were the First Guns that were Fired, and they were immediately followed by several volleys from the Regulars, by which Eight men, belonging to said Company, were killed, and several wounded.

Levi Harrington,
Levi Mead.

No. 11.Lexington, April 25, 1775.

I, William Draper, of lawful Age, and an Inhabitant of
Colrain, in the County of Hampshire, and Colony of
Massachusetts Bay, in New England, do testify and Declare,
that, being on the Parade of said Lexington, April 19th Instant,
about half an hour before sunrise, the King's Regular Troops
appeared at the meeting House of Lexington. Captain Parkers
Company, who were drawn up back of said meeting house on
the Parade, turned from said Troops, making their escape, by
dispersing; in the mean time, the Regular Troops made an
huzza, and ran towards Captain Parkers Company, who were
dispersing, and, immediately after the huzza was made, the
Commanding Officer of said troops (as I took him) gave the
command to the said troops, "fire! fire! damn you, fire!" and
immediately, they fired before any of Captain Parkers
Company fired, I then being within three or four Rods of said
Regular Troops: And further say not.

William Draper.[370]

No. 12. Lexington, April 23, 1775.

---

[370] Sworn to before William Reed, Josiah Johnson and William Stickney.

I, Thomas Fessenden, of Lawful age, testify and Declare, that,
being in a Pasture near the meeting house, at said Lexington,
on Wednesday last, at about half an hour before sunrise, I saw
a number of Regular troops pass speedily by said meeting
house, on their way towards a Company of Militia of said
Lexington, who were assembled to the number of about one
hundred in a company, at the Distance of eighteen or twenty
rods from said meeting house; and after they had passed by
said meeting house, I saw three Officers, on horseback,
advance to the front of said Regulars, when one of them, being
within six rods of the said Militia, cryed out, "Disperse, you
Rebels, immediately," on which he Brandished his sword over
his head three times; meanwhiles the second Officer, who was
about two rods behind him, fired a Pistol, pointed at said
Militia, and the Regulars kept huzzaing till he had finished
brandishing his sword, and when he had thus finished
brandishing his sword, he pointed it Down towards said
Militia, and immediately on which the said Regulars fired a
Volley at the Militia, and then I ran off as fast as I could,
while they continued firing, till I got out of their reach. I
further testify, that as soon as ever the officer Cryed
"Disperse, you rebels," the said Company of Militia dispersed
every way, as fast as they could, and, while they were
Dispersing, the regulars kept firing at them incessantly: And
further saith not.

Thomas Fessenden.

No. 13. Lincoln, April 23, 1775.

I, John Bateman, belonging to the fifty-second regiment,
commanded by Colonel Jones, on Wednesday morning, on the
nineteenth Day of April instant, was in the Party marching to
Concord, being at Lexington, in the County of Middlesex,
being nigh the meeting house in said Lexington, there was a
small party of men gathered together in that place, when our
said troops marched by, and I Testify and Declare, that I heard
the word of command given to the Troops to fire, and some of
said Troops Did fire, and I saw one of said small party lay
Dead on the ground nigh said meeting house; and I testify, that
I never heard any of the Inhabitants so much as fire one gun
on said Troops.

John Bateman.[371]

No. 14 Lexington, April 23, 1775.

---

[371] Sworn to before John Cummings and Duncan Ingraham.

We, John Hoar, John Whithead, Abraham Garfield, Benjamin Munroe, Isaac Parks, William Hosmer, John Adams, Gregory Stone, all of Lincoln, in the County of Middlesex, Massachusetts Bay, all of lawfull age, do testify and say, that, on Wednesday last, we were assembled at Concord, in the morning of said Day, in Consequence of information received, that a Brigade of Regular Troops were on their march to the said town of Concord, who had killed six men at the Town of Lexington; About an hour afterwards we saw them approaching, to the Number, as we Apprehended, of about Twelve hundred, on which we retreated to a Hill about Eighty Rods back, and the said Troops then took Possession of the Hill, where we were first Posted; presently after this, we saw the Troops moving towards the North Bridge, about one Mile from the said Concord Meeting House; we then immediately went before them and passed the Bridge just before a party of them, to the Number of about two hundred, arrived; They there left about one half of their two hundred at the Bridge, and proceeded, with the rest, towards Col. Barretts, about two Miles from the said Bridge; we then seeing several fires in the Town, thought the Houses in Concord were in danger, and Marched towards the said Bridge; and the Troops that were stationed there, observing our approach, marched back over the Bridge and then took up some of the Plank; we then hastened our March towards the Bridge, and when we had got near the Bridge, they fired on our men, first three Guns, one after the other, and then a Considerable Number more; and then, and not before (having orders from our Commanding Officers not to fire till we were fired upon) we fired upon the Regulars and they Retreated. On their Retreat through the Town of Lexington to Charlestown, they Ravaged and destroyed private property, and burnt three Houses one Barn and one Shop.

No. 15 Lexington, April 23, 1775.

We, Nathan Barrett, Captain; Jonathan Farrar, Joseph Butler, and Francis Wheeler, Lieutenants; John Barrett, Ensign; John Brown, Silas Walker, Ephraim Melvin, Nathan Buttrick, Stephen Hosmer, Junr. Samuel Barrett, Thomas Jones, Joseph Chandler, Peter Wheeler, Nathan Peirce, and Edward Richardson, all of Concord, in the County of Middlesex, in the province of the Massachusetts Bay, of Lawfull Age, Testify and Declare, that on Wednesday, the Nineteenth Instant, about an Hour after sun rise, we Assembled on a Hill near the meeting House, in Concord aforesaid, in consequence of an information, that a number of regular Troops had killed six of our Countrymen, at Lexington, and were on their march to said Concord; and about an Hour afterwards, we saw them approaching, to the number, as we Imagine, of about Twelve Hundred; on which we retreated to a Hill about Eighty rods back, and the aforesaid Troops then took possession of a Hill where we were first posted. Presently after this, we saw them moving towards the North Bridge, about one mile from the said meeting House; we then immediately went before them, and passed the bridge just before a party of them, to the number of about Two Hundred, arrived. They there left about one half of these two Hundred at the bridge, and proceeded with the rest towards Colonel Barret's, about two miles from the said bridge. We then seing several fires in the Town, thought our houses were in Danger, and immediately march'd back towards said bridge, and the troops who were station'd there, observing our approach, march'd back over the bridge, and then took up some of the planks. We then hastened our Steps towards the bridge, and when we had got near the bridge, they fir'd on our men, first three guns, one after the other, and then a Considerable number more; upon which, and not before, (having orders from our Commanding Officer not to fire till we were fired upon) we fir'd upon the regulars, and they retreated. At Concord, and on their retreat thro' Lexington, they plunder'd many houses, burnt three at Lexington, together with a shop and barn, and committed damage, more or less, to almost every House from Concord to Charlestown.

[Signed by the above deponents.]

We, Joseph Butler, and Ephraim Melvin, do testify and declare, that when the regular troops fir'd upon our people, at the North Bridge, in Concord, as related in the foregoing depositions, they shot one, and we believe two, of our people before we fir'd a single gun at them.

Joseph Butler,
Ephraim Melvin.[372]

APPENDIX K

---

[372] Sworn to before Jonathan Hastings, John Cummings and Duncan Ingraham.

JONAS PARKER

Jonas Parker's ties to Colonial Massachusetts can be traced back to his ancestor Thomas Parker, who departed from London, England on March 11, 1635. Upon arrival in Massachusetts Bay Colony, Thomas initially settled in Lynn. His family later established residence in Reading. On August 3, 1664, Jonas' grandfather John Parker was born. John married twice, first to a Deliverance Dodge of Beverly and second to a woman only known as "Sarah". The first marriage produced eight children, including Jonas' father Andrew. The second marriage none. All of the children were born in Reading.

On June 25, 1712, John Parker purchased land in the southern part of Cambridge Farms from a John Cutler. The property was described as "one small Mansion house and about sixty Acres of Land more or less, and is bounded - Southerly upon sd Watertown Line."[373] He and his family subsequently settled on the property.

John Parker and his son Andrew served as the town's "fence viewers" and constables.[374] It appears that in the early 18th Century the family was very prominent, as the Parkers occupied the second row of pews in the town meeting house.[375]

---

[373] Charles Hudson, History of the Town of Lexington. Genealogies, Vol. II, (Boston: Houghton Mifflin Company, 1913), 507.

[374] In Massachusetts, the post of "fence viewer" was first established in 1693 by a statute which was amended in 1785 and again in 1836. Early Fence Viewers, armed with wall measurements, were able to arbitrate and/or prosecute such crimes by adjoining farmers. Trespassing by livestock was illegal. Boundaries and fences had to be maintained. If a farmer neglected his fence, his neighbor could do the repairs and charge his nonperforming neighbor twice the cost. If the negligent neighbor didn't come up with the money, he had to pay 12% interest until payment was made.

[375] Ibid. Other prominent families that were seated near the Parkers included the Masons and Meads

On August 2, 1720, Jonas' father married Sarah Whitney, the daughter of Isaiah and Sarah Whitney. Jonas Parker was born in Lexington on February 6, 1721 along with his twin sister Sarah. The twins were the oldest of twelve children. In total, he had seven sisters and four brothers. On June 30, 1745, the Parker and Munroe families united when Jonas married Lucy Munroe. At the time of the wedding, Lucy was already pregnant with their first child.[376] Lucy was born on October 9, 1745. Sadly, she was born "deaf and dumb". By 1761, Jonas and Lucy had nine more children. Four were boys, the remaining six were girls. In 1775, the oldest child was thirty years old, the youngest, Mary, was fourteen.[377]

Primary and secondary sources indicate Jonas and his family resided on Bedford Road north of the Lexington Common and immediately next door to the Reverend Jonas Clarke. A review of Jonas' estate inventory supports the proposition he was both a woodworker and yeoman by trade. Some of the tools and materials owned by him on the eve of the Battle of Lexington included "Ruff timber in the shop, 5 hubs and spokes for woollen wheels, Timber for foot wheels, turned timber for wheels, 54 feet of joyce, 2 new screws, 2 lathes, New beadstead, Screw bench [and] wooden vice."[378] Parker appears to also be an avid reader as he owned a "Psalm book, old bible [and a] number of other books."[379] Jonas, like his younger brother Amos, was described as a tall man with

---

[376] According to Robert Gross, on the eve of the American Revolution one out of three first born children were conceived out of wedlock. From the 1740's onward, births less than nine months after marriage steadily increased. In the 1740's, nineteen percent of all first births were prenuptial conceptions. By 1774, forty-one percent of all first borns were conceived out of wedlock. Robert Gross, The Minutemen and Their World, (New York: Hill and Wang, 1976), 100. See also note 59.

[377] Lucy, Prudence, Elizabeth and Mary still resided with Jonas and his wife in 1775.

[378] Estate of Jonas Parker, April 11, 1788.

[379] Ibid.

great strength. He was considered the best wrestler in the town.[380]

Unfortunately for Jonas, his financial status in Lexington was significantly lower than that of his father and grandfather. Although Parker was not poor, he was not wealthy either. A review of Lexington's tax valuations of 1774 reveals Jonas' personal and real property was taxed at a rate of two shillings, eleven pence.[381] By comparison, the wealthiest resident of Lexington, William Reed, Esq., was assessed 16 shillings, one pence. The town's poorest resident, Ephraim Winship, was assessed a mere ten pence.[382]

Although there are no records of Jonas Parker serving at the Siege of Louisbourg or the French and Indian Wars, he was certainly a member of the town's militia company.

By 1775, Parker, like many of his neighbors, believed war with the Crown was inevitable. In the days leading up to the Battle of Lexington, Parker openly expressed his intent to fight if hostilities broke out. According to Elijah Sanderson, "some days before the Battle, I was conversing with Jonas Parker, who was killed, and heard him express his determination never to run from before the British troops."[383]

Given Jonas Parker's close proximity to both the Lexington Common and the Reverend Clarke's residence, it is

---

[380]

https://archive.org/stream/genealogybiograp00park/genealogybiograp00par k_djvu.txt

[381] Town of Lexington Tax Valuation Rolls, 1774.

[382] Ibid. The decrease in Parker's financial worth was due to an increase in Lexington's population prior to the war coupled with a fixed supply of land available to inheriting sons. As a result, many young men in Lexington were forced to seek land north or west of Lexington, purchase smaller tracts of land inside Lexington or share with their brothers a divided inheritance.

[383] Deposition of Elijah Sanderson, December 17, 1824.

likely he assembled with other elements of the Training Band after Paul Revere's arrival in Lexington. Whether Jonas remained at Buckman Tavern or returned home after the company was dismissed is unknown.

When the Training Band reassembled hours later for the Battle of Lexington, Jonas Parker was present. Also on the Common with him was his son Jonas, Jr., his first cousins John and Thaddeus Parker and his nephew Ebenezer Parker. Other relatives in the ranks included Ensign Robert Munroe, Samuel Munroe, Jedediah Munroe, John Munroe, Stephen Munroe, Stephen Munroe Jr., Ebenezer Munroe, Nathan Munroe, Edmund Munroe and Sergeant William Munroe.

According to Jonas' son, "on the Morning of the Nineteenth of April Instant, about one or two o'clock, being informed, that a Number of Regular Officers had been Riding up and down the Road the evening and night preceding, and that some of the Inhabitants, as they were passing, had been Insulted by the Officers, and stopped by them; and being also Informed, that the Regular Troops were on their March from Boston, in order (as it was said) to take the Colony Stores, then Deposited at Concord, we met on the Parade of our Company in this town; After the Company had Collected, we were Ordered, by Captain Parker, (who Commanded us) to Disperse for the Present, and to be Ready to attend the beat of the Drum, and Accordingly the Company went into houses near the place of Parade. We further Testify and Say, that, about five o'Clock in the morning, we attended the beat of our Drum, and were formed on the Parade; we were faced towards the Regulars then marching up to us, and some of our Company were comeing to the parade with their backs towards the Troops, and Others on the parade, began to Disperse when the Regulars fired on the Company, before a Gun was fired by any of our company on them. They killed eight of our company, and wounded several, and continued their fire, until we had all made our escape."

True to his earlier pledge to Elijah Sanderson, Jonas Parker stood his ground when hostilities erupted on the Lexington Common. After the British light infantry opened fire, they "made a huzza" and ran furiously towards the retiring militia.[384] As the soldiers surged forward, Ebenezer Munroe remembered Jonas Parker "standing . . .with his balls and flints in his hat, on the ground between his feet, and heard him declare he would never run. He was shot down at the second fire . . . I saw him struggling on the ground, attempting to load his gun . . .As he lay on the ground, they [ran] him through with the bayonet."[385]

As the regulars left the onslaught behind them, wives, children and the spectators emerged from hiding and made their way onto the common. Many were overcome with emotion and grief at the sight of husbands, sons, brothers, cousins and neighbors lying dead or wounded on the field. As they began to tend to the wounded, over two hundred men from Woburn's militia and minuteman companies arrived in Lexington. Disturbed at what they saw, the men halted and assisted the Lexington residents in treating the wounded and carrying the dead into the meetinghouse. Afterwards, the Woburn men reassembled and resumed their march toward Concord.[386]

---

[384] Deposition of Captain John Parker, April 25, 1775; Deposition of William Draper, April 25, 1775. "The balls flew so thick, I thought there was no chance for escape." Deposition of Ebenezer Munroe, April 2, 1825.

[385] Deposition of Ebenezer Munroe, April 2, 1825. If this deposition is assumed to be accurate, then the reference to "balls and flint in his hat" suggests it is likely that Jonas Parker may have fielded at the Battle of Lexington with a shot pouch and horn instead of a cartridge pouch.

[386] According to Major Loammi Baldwin of Woburn, "We mustered as fast as possible. The Town turned out extra-ordinary, and proceeded toward Lexington . . . I rode along a little before the main body, and when I was nigh Jacob Reed's I heard a great firing; proceeded on, soon heard that the Regulars had fired upon Lexington people and killed a large number of them. We proceeded on as fast as possible and came to Lexington and saw about eight or ten dead and numbers wounded."

The Reverend Clarke's daughter, Elizabeth, described the original burial of Jonas Parker and the seven other men killed at the Battle of Lexington. "Father sent Jonas down to Grandfather Cook's to see who was killed and what their condition was and, in the afternoon, Father, Mother with me and the baby went to the Meeting House. There was the eight men that was killed, seven of them my Father's parishioners, one from Woburn, all in Boxes made of four large boards nailed up and, after Pa had prayed, they were put into two horse carts and took into the grave yard where some of the neighbors had made a large trench, as near the woods as possible and there we followed the bodies of those first slain, Father, Mother, I and the baby, there I stood and there I saw them let down into the ground, it was a little rainy but we waited to see them covered up with clods and then for fear the British should find them, my Father thought some of the men had best cut some pine or oak bows and spread them on their place of burial so that it looked like a heap of brush."[387]

Following Jonas' death, the remaining members of the Parker family who lived in Lexington struggled to stay intact. It is possible that Jonas' wife either passed away in 1778 or became incapable of caring for Lucy and the two youngest Parker girls, Elizabeth and Mary. That same year, guardians were appointed to care for the three young women. Lucy and Elizabeth left Lexington to live with their guardians in Princeton (MA) and Billerica respectively. Dr. Joseph Fiske was appointed guardian of Mary. She remained in Lexington until her marriage in 1782.[388]

For unknown reasons, Jonas's estate was not probated

---

[387] Elizabeth Clarke to Lucy Allen, April 20, 1835. Elizabeth was twelve years old at the Battle of Lexington.
[388] Charles Hudson, History of the Town of Lexington, 509.

in the Middlesex Courts until 1788. A partial review of his estate reveals the following items and their respective value:

> Ruff timber in the shop, kitchen chamber 0 4 7 0
> small sugar box, 2 great buttery, toster 0 2 0 0
> 5 hubs and spokes for woollen wheels 0 4 7 3
> Timber for foot wheels, part wrought 0 10 4 3
> turned timber for wheels, foot wheel __?__ 0 14 8 0
> 54 feet of joyce, 2 new screws in the shop 0 7 8 3
> New beadstead in the shop ___?___ 0 7 0 0
> Blue great coat, blue strait bodied coat 2 15 4 0
> Camblet coat, pair of knit breeches 1 3 4 0
> Green jacket, white jacket, dark sustion coat 0 9 2 0
> Gray wooling coat, stript lining, wooll jacket 0 7 4 0
> Leather breeches, fine shirt 0 10 0 0
> Silk handkerchief, lowered pocket handkerchief 0 3 0 1
> Cheked handkerchief, bewer hat, wigglet 0 12 4 0
> Pr calf skin shoes 0 7 4 0
> Blue tow stockings, blue grey stockings 0 3 8 0
> Pr of leggings, read cap, pr of new gloves 0 3 0 1
> Yearling calf, burrow, a sow 3 8 0 0
> 2 woollen spinning wheels, foot wheel 0 16 8 0
> 5 earthen plates and 2 earthen bowls 0 1 4 3
> Psalm book, old bible, number of other books 0 2 7 3
> Small hollow plain, 2 lathes 0 9 8 0
> Screw bench, wooden vice 0 7 10 1
> Barrel tub, 2 washing tubs 0 2 1 2[389]

On the 60th Anniversary of the Battle of Lexington, Jonas Parker and the other seven men killed at the engagement were removed from the town's burial ground and reinterred in a ceremonial vault located underneath the oldest monument on the Lexington Common.[390] During the ceremony it was the

---

[389] Estate of Jonas Parker, April 11, 1788
[390] The monument itself was dedicated in 1799. The powerful inscription on the monument was written by Parker's neighbor, the Reverend Clarke.

famed statesmen Edward Everett who highlighted the sacrifice and courage of Jonas Parker. At the height of his speech, he simply declared "History, — Roman history, — does not furnish an example of bravery that out shines that of Jonas Parker. A truer heart did not bleed at Thermopylae."[391]

The inscription reads: *"The Blood of these Martyr's In the cause of God & their Country, Was the Cement of the Union of these States, then Colonies; & gave the spring to the spirit. Firmness And resolution of their Fellow Citizens. They rose as one man to revenge their brethren's Blood and at the point of the sword to assert; Defend their native Rights. They nobly dar'd to be free!!"*

[391] Edward Everett, An Address Delivered at Lexington on the 19th (20th) of April, 1835, (Charlestown, 1835), 22.

APPENDIX L

THE OFFICIAL TITLE OF THE LEXINGTON MILITIA

As discussed in this book, Lexington's militia was not known in 1775 as the "Lexington Minute Men". Available research suggests a formal minute company had yet to be established by April, 1775. This is not to say that the town made no effort to establish a minute company. On December 28, 1774, the town voted "to provide bayonets at the town's cost for one third of the training soldiers."[392] However, other period accounts, including the correspondence from the Reverend William Gordon, suggest the Lexington militia was only divided into two bodies: The Training Band and Alarm List. A minute company simply did not exist in Lexington.

The Lexington Alarm List would have been composed of men over the age of sixty and served as a reserve to the Training Band. Period documents from the town support the proposition that its militia was *officially known* as "Training Band" and its soldiers were called "training soldiers". For example, In November of 1774, the selectmen of the town voted to tax itself "forty pounds for the purpose of mounting cannon, ammunition, for a pair of drums for the use of the Training Band in the town and for carriage and harness for burying the dead."[393]

However, depositions from some of the Lexington militiamen in the aftermath of the Battle of Lexington informally referred to their town militia not as the Lexington Training Band, but as "Captain Parker's Company". On April 25, 1775, Simon Winship stated the British troops "marched on till they came within a few Rods of Captain Parkers

---

[392] Declarations and Resolves, Town of Lexington, December 28, 1774.
[393] Lexington Town Records, November 10 - December 27, 1774, Lexington Town Hall.

Company."[394] A day earlier, John Robbins asserted "that on the Nineteenth Instant, the Company under the Command of Captain John Parker, being drawn up (sometime before sun Rise) on the Green or Common."[395] William Draper stated "I, William Draper, of lawful Age, and an Inhabitant of Colrain, in the County of Hampshire, and Colony of Massachusetts Bay, in New England, do testify and Declare, that, being on the Parade of said Lexington, April 19th Instant, about half an hour before sunrise, the King's Regular Troops appeared at the meeting House of Lexington. Captain Parkers Company, who were drawn up back of said meeting house on the Parade, turned from said Troops, making their escape, by dispersing; in the meantime, the Regular Troops made an huzza, and ran towards Captain Parkers Company."[396]

Surprisingly, a third name, "Lexington Company", was also utilized by the town's militiamen. In other depositions immediately following the Battle of Lexington, no less than five Lexington men refer to their unit as "The Lexington Company". "I, Elijah Saunderson, above named, do further testifie and declare, that I was on Lexington Common, the Morning of the Nineteenth of April, aforesaid, having been dismissed by the Officers above mentioned, and saw a Large Body of Regular Troops advancing toward Lexington Company."[397] According to Benjamin Tidd, "the regulars fired, first, a few guns, which we took to be pistols from some of the Regulars who were mounted on Horses, and then the said Regulars fired a Volley or two before any guns were fired by the Lexington Company."[398] Finally, Timothy Smith recalled "I saw a large body of regular troops marching up towards the Lexington company, then dispersing, and likewise saw the regular troops fire on the Lexington company, before

---

[394] Deposition of Simon Wisnship, April 25, 1775.
[395] Deposition of John Robbins, April 24, 1775.
[396] Deposition of William Draper, April 25, 1775.
[397] Deposition of Elijah Sanderson, April 25, 1775.
[398] Deposition of Benjamin Tidd, April 25, 1775.

the latter fired a gun; I immediately ran, and a volley was discharged at me, which put me in imminent danger of losing my life; I soon returned to the Common, and saw eight of the Lexington men who were killed, and lay bleeding at a considerable distance from each other; and several were wounded: And further saith not."[399]

Thus, given the above, confusion still remains as to the official title of the Lexington militia that fought at the Battle of Lexington. Town records refer to the company as "The Training Band. That said, it was not outside the realm of possibility that many members of the organization commonly referred to themselves informally as "The Lexington Company" or "Captain Parker's Company". As a result, all three names are proper references to the militia unit that fought at the Battle of Lexington.

---

[399] Deposition of Timothy Smith, April 25, 1775.

APPENDIX M

SERMON DELIVERED BY THE REVEREND JONAS
CLARKE COMMEMORATING THE FIRST
ANNIVERSARY OF THE BATTLE OF LEXINGTON

"On the evening of the 18th of April, 1775, we received two
messages--the first verbal, the other, by express, in writing--
from the Committee of Safety, who were then sitting in
the westerly part of Cambridge, directed to the Honorable
John Hancock, Esq., who, with the Honorable Samuel Adams,
Esq., was then providentially with us, informing that eight
or nine officers of the king's troops were seen just before night
passing the road towards Lexington in a musing,
contemplative posture; and it was suspected they were out
upon some evil design. Both these gentlemen had been
frequently, and even publicly, threatened by the enemies of
this people, both in England and America, with the vengeance
of the British administration. And as Mr. Hancock, in
particular, had been more than once personally insulted by
some officers of the troops in Boston, it was not without some
just grounds supposed that under coverage of the darkness,
sudden arrest--if not assassination--might be attempted by
these instruments of tyranny. To prevent anything of this
kind, ten or twelve men were immediately collected in arms to
guard my house through the night.

In the meantime, said officers passed through this town on the
road towards Concord. It was, therefore, thought expedient to
watch their motions and, if possible, make some
discovery of their intentions. Accordingly, about ten o'clock
in the evening, three men on horses were dispatched for this
purpose. As they were peaceably passing the road
towards Concord and the borders of Lincoln, they were
suddenly stopped by said officers, who rode up to them, and,

putting pistols to their breasts and seizing their horses' bridles,
swore if they stirred another step, they should be all dead men.
The officers detained them several hours as prisoners,
examined, searched, abused, and insulted them; and in their
hasty return, supposing themselves discovered, they left them
in Lexington. Said officers also took into custody, abused,
and threatened with their lives, several other persons, some of
whom they met peaceably passing on the road; others, even at
the doors of their dwellings, without the least provocation on
the part of the inhabitants, or so much as a question asked by
them.

Between the hours of twelve and one on the morning of the
19th of April, we received intelligence, by express, from the
intelligence service, the Honorable Joseph Warren, Esq.
at Boston, that a large body of the king's troops, supposed to
be a brigade of about twelve or fifteen hundred, were
embarked in boats from Boston and gone over to land on Lake
Marispoint ,so-called, in Cambridge. It was shrewdly
suspected that they were ordered to seize and destroy the
stores of arms belonging to the colony, then deposited at
Concord, in consequence of General Gage's unjustifiable
seizure of the provincial magazine of powder at Medford, and
other colony stores, in several other places.

Upon this timely intelligence, the militia of this town were
alarmed, and ordered to meet on the usual place of parade.
This, this was not with any design of commencing
hostilities upon the king's troops, but to consult what might be
done for our own and the people's safety; and also, to be ready
for whatever service Providence might call us out to upon this
alarming occasion, in case--just in case--overt acts of violence
or open hostilities should be committed by this mercenary
band of armed and blood-thirsty oppressors.

About the same time, two persons were sent, express, to
Cambridge, if possible to gain intelligence of the motions of

the troops and what route they took. The militia met,
according to order, and waited the return of the messengers
that they might order their measures as occasion should
require. Between three and four o'clock, one of the expresses
returned, informing that there was no appearance of the troops
on the roads to Cambridge and Charlestown and that the
movements of the army were but a feint to alarm the people.
Upon this, therefore, the militia company were dismissed for
the present, but with orders to be within call of the drum,
waiting the return of the other messenger who was expected in
about an hour, or sooner, if any discovery should be made of
the motions of the troops.

But he was prevented by their silent and sudden arrival at the
place where he was waiting for intelligence, so that, after all
this precaution, we had no notice of their approach till
the brigade was actually, actually in the town, and upon a
quick march, within about a mile and a quarter of the meeting
house and place of parade. However, the commanding officer
thought best to call the company together, not with any
design of opposing so superior a force, much less of
commencing hostilities, but only with a view to determine
what to do, when and where to meet, and to dismiss and
disperse. Accordingly, about half an hour after four o'clock,
alarm guns were fired, and the drums beat to-arms, and the
militia were collecting together; some to the number of about
fifty or sixty or possibly more were on the parade; others were
coming towards it.

In the meantime, the troops, having thus stolen a march upon
us, to prevent any intelligence of their approach, seized and
held prisoners several persons whom they met
unarmed upon the road. They seemed to come determined for
murder and bloodshed; and that, whether provoked to it or not.

When within about half a quarter of a mile of the meeting
house they halted, and the command was given to prime and
load, which, being done, they marched on till they

came up to the east end of said meeting house, in sight of our
militia, collecting us aforesaid, who were about twelve or
thirteen rods distant. Immediately upon their appearing so
suddenly and so nigh, Captain Parker, who commanded the
militia company, ordered the men to disperse, and take care of
themselves, and not to fire. Upon this, our men dispersed, but
many of them not so speedily as they might have done, not
having the most distant idea of such brutal barbarity, and more
than savage cruelty, from the troops of a British king as they
immediately experienced. For no sooner did they come in
sight of our company, but one of them, supposed to be an
officer of rank, was heard to say to the troops: 'Damn them!
We will have them' Upon which, the troops shouted aloud,
and huzzah-ed, and rushed furiously toward our men.

About this same time, three officers, supposed to be Colonel
Smith, Major Pitcairn, and another officer, advanced on
horseback to the front of the body, and coming within five
or six rods of the militia, one of them cried out: 'Ye villains!
Ye rebels! Disperse, damn you! Disperse!' or words to this
effect. One of them, whether the same or not is not easily
determined, said: 'Lay down your arms! Damn you! Why
don't you lay down your arms?!' The second of these officers,
about this time, fired a pistol towards the militia as they were
dispersing. The foremost, who was within a few yards of our
men, brandishing his sword, and then pointing towards them,
with a loud voice said to the troops: 'Fire! By God, fire!'--
which was instantly followed by discharge of arms from
the said troops, succeeded by a very heavy and close fire upon
our dispersing party, so long as any of them were within reach.

Eight were left dead upon the ground. Ten were wounded.

The rest of the company, through Divine goodness, were, to a
miracle, preserved unhurt in this murderous action.

Having thus vanquished the party in Lexington, the troops
marched on for Concord, to execute their orders in destroying

the stores belonging to the colony deposited there. They met with no interruption in their march to Concord; but by some means or other, the people of Concord had notice of their approach and designs, and were alarmed about break of day; and collecting as soon and as many as possible, improved the time they had before the troops came upon them to the best advantage, both for concealing and securing as many of the public stores as they could, and in preparing for defense.

By the stop of the troops at Lexington, many thousands were saved to the colony, and they were, in a great measure, frustrated in their design. When the troops made their approach to the easterly part of the town, the provincials of Concord and some neighboring towns were collected, and collecting, in an advantageous post on a hill just a little distance from the meeting house north of the road, to the number of about 150 or maybe 200. But finding the troops to be more than three times as many, they very wisely retreated, first to a hill about 80 rods further north, and then over the North Bridge--so-called--about a mile from the town. And there they waited the coming of the militia of the towns adjacent to their assistance. They spied the British in the distance. The British detachment marched into the center of the town.

A party of about 200 was ordered to take possession of said bridge; other parties were dispatched to various parts of the town in search of public stores; while the remainder were employed in seizing and destroying whatever they could find in the townhouse and other places where stores had been lodged. But before they had accomplished their design, they were interrupted by a discharge of arms at said bridge. The provincials, who were in sight of the bridge, observing the troops attempting to take up the planks of said bridge, thought it necessary to dislodge them. They accordingly marched, but with express orders not to fire unless first fired upon by the king's troops. Upon their approach towards the bridge, Captain Laurie's party fired upon them; killed Captain Davis

and another man upon the spot; and wounded several others.
Upon this, our militia rushed on, with the spirit becoming
freeborn Americans, returned the fire upon the enemy; killed
two; wounded several; and drove them from the bridge; and
pursued them towards the town till they were covered by a re-
enforcement from the main body.

The provincials then took post on a hill at some distance north
of the town and, as their numbers were continually increasing,
they were preparing to give the troops a proper discharge on
their departure from the town. In the meantime, the king's
troops collected; and having dressed their wounded, destroyed
what stores they could find, and insulted and plundered a
number of the inhabitants, prepared for a retreat.

The troops began a hasty retreat about the middle of the day,
and were no sooner out of the town but they began to meet the
effects of the just resentments of this injured people. The
provincials fired upon them from various quarters and pursued
them, though without any military order, with a firmness and
intrepidity beyond what could have been expected on the first
onset, and in such a day of confusion in distress.

The fire was returned for a time with great fury by the troops
as they retreated, though through Divine goodness, but with
little execution, this scene continued with but little
intermission till they returned to Lexington, when it was
evident that, having lost numbers in killed, wounded, and
prisoners that fell into our hands, they began to be not
only fatigued, but greatly disheartened. And it is supposed
that they must have soon surrendered at discretion had they
not been re-enforced.

But Lord Percy's arrival, with another brigade of about a
thousand men and two field pieces about half a mile from
Lexington meetinghouse towards Cambridge, gave them a
seasonable respite. The coming of this re-enforcement with
the cannon, which our people were not so well acquainted

with then as they have been since, brought the provincials also to a pause for a time. But no sooner were the king's troops in motion but our men renewed the pursuit with equal and even greater ardor and intrepidity than before. The firing on both sides continued with but little intermission to the close of the day, when the troops entered Charlestown where the provincials could not follow them without exposing the worthy inhabitants of that truly patriotic town to their rage and revenge.

That night and the next day, they were conveyed in boats over Charles River to Boston, glad to secure themselves under the cover of the shipping, and by strengthening and perfecting the fortifications at every part against the further attacks of a justly incensed people, who upon intelligence of the murderous transactions of this fatal day, were collecting in arms around the town in great numbers, and from every quarter.

In the retreat of the king's troops from Concord to Lexington, they ravaged and plundered as they had opportunity more or less in most of the houses that were upon the road. But after they were joined by Percy's brigade in Lexington, it seemed as if all the little remains of humanity had left them, and rage--rage--and revenge had taken the reins and knew no bounds. Clothing, furniture, provisions, goods: plundered, broken, carried off, or destroyed. Buildings, especially dwelling houses: abused, defaced, battered, shattered, and indeed, almost ruined. And as if this had not been enough, numbers of them doomed to the flames: free dwelling houses, two shops, and a barn were laid in ashes in Lexington. Many others were set on fire in this town, in Cambridge, etc., and must have shared the same fate had not the close pursuit of the provincials prevented and the flames been seasonably quenched. Add to all this the unarmed, the aged and infirm, who were unable to flee, were inhumanely stabbed and murdered in their habitations. Yes, even women in childbed, with their helpless babes in their

arms, did not escape the horrid alternative of either being
cruelly murdered in their beds, burnt in their habitations,
or turned into the streets to perish with cold, nakedness, and
distress. But I forebear; for words are too insignificant to
express the horrid barbarities of that distressing day.

Our loss in several actions of that day was 49 killed, 34
wounded, and 5 missing who were taken prisoners and have
since been exchanged. The enemy's loss, according to the
best accounts of killed, wounded, and missing: about 300."

APPENDIX N

COMPANY COMMANDERS OF LIEUTENANT COLONEL LOAMMI BALDWIN'S (LATE COLONEL GERRISH'S) 38TH REGIMENT, AUGUST 1775

Company	*Company Commander*
1st Company	Thomas Mighill
2nd Company	Barnabus Dodge
3d Company	Richard Dodge
4th Company	Isaac Sherman
5th Company	John Wood
6th Company	Thomas Cogswell
7th Company	Timothy Corey
8th Company	William Rogers
9th Company	Samuel Sprague
10th Company	Joseph Pettingill

BIBLIOGRAPHY

A. Primary Sources

1. Journals

Journal of Seth Metcalf, April 25, 1757, December 30, 1795.

Journal of Joseph Nichols, June 6, 1758, June 8, 1758, June 24, 1758, August 9, 1758, September 3, 1758.

Journal of Caleb Rea, July 10, 1758.

Journal of Arthur Harris of the Bridgewater Coy of Militia.

Diary of Lt. Frederick Mackenzie, Royal Welsh Fusiliers.

Henry De Berniere, *Narrative of Occurrences, 1775*, (Boston, 1779)

2. Instructions, Resolves and Reports

"Instructions from Jonas Clarke to William Reed Esq., the Present Representative of Lexington, October 21, 1765."

Declarations and Resolves, Town of Lexington, October 21, 1765.

Declarations and Resolves, Town of Lexington, December 28, 1767.

Declarations and Resolves, Town of Lexington, September 21, 1768.

Declarations and Resolves, Town of Lexington, January 5, 1773.

Report of the Committee of Correspondence adopted by the Town of Lexington, December 1773.

Declarations and Resolves, Town of Lexington, September 26, 1774.

Report of the Committee Appointed by the Town of Andover, November 14, 1774.

Town of Roxbury Resolves, December 26, 1774.

Declarations and Resolves, Town of Lexington, December 28, 1774.

Town of Braintree Resolves, January 23, 1775.

Orders from General Thomas Gage to Lieutenant-Colonel Francis Smith, 10th Regiment of Foot, April 18, 1775.

Report of Lieutenant-Colonel Smith to General Gage, April 22, 1775.

General Orders of George Washington, August 17, 1775.

General orders of George Washington, August 19, 1775

Report of Loammi Baldwin to George Washington, August 2, 1775.

Report of Loammi Baldwin to George Washington, September 15, 1775.

Report of Loammi Baldwin to George Washington, October 1, 1775.

3. Letters

Letter from Lieutenant Governor Hutchinson to Richard Jackson, August 30, 1765.

Letter from Governor Bernard to Shelburne, March 19, 1768.

Letter from Hugh Earle Percy to the Duke of Northumberland, July 27, 1774.

Letter from Hugh Earle Percy to the Duke of Northumberland, September 12, 1774.

Letter from Hugh Earle Percy to General Harvey, April 20, 1775.

Letter from Brigadier General Hugh Earle Percy to General Gage, April 20, 1775.

Letter from Major Pitcairn to General Gage, April 26, 1775.

Letter from Lt. William Sutherland to Major Kemble, April 27, 1775.

"An account of the commencement of Hostilities between Great Britain and America, in the Province of the Massachusetts-Bay. By the Reverend Mr. William Gordon of Roxbury, in a Letter to a Gentlemen in England, dated May 17, 1775."

Circular Letter to the Selectmen of Stoughtonham, July 6, 1775.

Letter from Joseph Reed to Samuel Garish, July 13, 1775.

4. Depositions

Deposition of William Woolton, March 18, 1768.

Deposition of John Bateman, April 23, 1775.

Deposition of Thomas Fessenden, April 23, 1775.

Depositions of Thomas Rice Willard, April 23, 1775.

Deposition of John Robins, April 24, 1775.

Draft Deposition of Paul Revere, April 24, 1775.

Deposition of Nathaniel Mulliken, April 25, 1775.

Depositions of Elijah Sanderson, Solomon Brown and Jonathan Loring, April 25, 1775.

Deposition of William Draper, April 25, 1775.

Deposition of John Parker, April 25, 1775.

Deposition of Timothy Smith, April 25, 1775.

Deposition of Simon Winship, April 25, 1775.

Deposition of Sergeant William Munroe, April 25, 1822.

Deposition of Elijah Sanderson, December 17, 1824.

Deposition of Nathan Munroe, December 22, 1824.

Deposition of Ebenezer Munroe, April 2, 1825.

221

Deposition of Sylvanus Wood, June 17, 1826.

5. Minutes of the Massachusetts Provincial Congress

Massachusetts Provincial Congress, Wednesday, October 5, 1774.

Massachusetts Provincial Congress, Wednesday, October 26, 1774.

Massachusetts Provincial Congress, Saturday, October 29, 1774.

Massachusetts Provincial Congress, April 23, 1775.

Massachusetts Provincial Congress, July 5, 1775.

6. Militia Laws, Muster Rolls and Drills

Commonwealth of Massachusetts, *Massachusetts Soldiers and Sailors of the American Revolution, Boston.*

Massachusetts Militia Laws, Nov. 22, 1693.

Pickering, Timothy *An Easy Plan of Discipline for a Militia*, Salem, 1775.

George Townshend, *A Plan of Discipline Composed for the Use of the Militia of the County of Norfolk*, London, 1759.

7. Newspaper Advertisements and Broadsides

S.C. Drake, *A List of the Names of the Provincials Who Were Killed in the Late Engagement With His*

Majesty's Troops at Concord &c,, May, 1775.

Isaiah Thomas, *A Narrative, of the Excursion and Ravages of the King's Troops Under the Command of General Gage, On the nineteenth of April, 1775. Together with the Depositions Taken by Order of Congress, to support the Truth of it.* Worcester, 1775

Continental Journal and Weekly Adviser, January 22, 1778.

Boston Gazette, May 26, 1777.

8. Sermons

"A Brief Narrative of the Principle Transactions of That Day" by Jonas Clarke, A.M., Pastor of the Church in Lexington, Massachusetts State, April19, 1776.

"A Sermon Preached Before His Excellency, John Hancock", Jonas Clarke, 1781.

9. Legal Treatises

Sir William Blackstone, *Commentaries on the Laws of England.* London 1765-1769.

B. Secondary Sources

Anderson, Fred, *A People's Army: Massachusetts Soldiers and Society in the Seven Years War*, London, England: W.W. Norton and Company, 1984.

Bolton, Charles K., *Letters of Hugh Earl Percy from Boston and New York*, Boston, Massachusetts: Charles E. Goodspeed, 1902.

Cain, Alexander R., *We Stood Our Ground: Lexington in the First Year of the American Revolution*, North Andover, Massachusetts: unpublished, 1995.

Chase, G.W., *History of Haverhill*, Haverhill, Massachusetts: self-published, 1861.

Cooke IV, Henry M., *Knapsacks, Snapsacks, Tumplines: Systems for Carrying Food and Clothing Used by Citizens and Soldeirs in 1775*, Randolph, Massachusetts: unpublished and undated.

-------, *The Massachusetts Bounty Coat of 1775*, Randolph, Massachusetts: unpublished and undated.

Darling, Anthony, *Red Coat and Brown Bess*, Alexandria Bay, New York: Museum Restoration Service, 1993.

Earle, Alice Morse, *Home Life in Colonial Days*, Stockbridge, Massachusetts: House Publishers, 1898.

Fischer, David Hackett, *Paul Revere's Ride*, New York, New York: Oxford University Press, 1994.

Frothingham, Richard , *History of the Siege of Boston and of the Battles of Lexington, Concord and Bunkerhill*, Boston, Massachusetts: Little, Brown and Company, 1849.

Galvin, John R., *The Minute Men The First Fight: Myths and Realities of the American Revolution*, Washington D.C.: Brassey's Inc., 1989.

Gilgun, Beth, *Tidings from the 18th Century*, Texarkana, Texas: Rebel Publishing, 1993.

Gross, Robert, *The Minute Men and Their World*, New York, New York: Hill and Wang, 1976.

Harris, Edward M., *Andover in the American Revolution*, Marceline, Missouri: Walsworth Publishing Company, 1976.

Hibbert, Christopher, *Red Coats and Rebels: The American Revolution Through British Eyes*, New York, New York: Avon Books, 1990.

Hudson, Charles S., *History of the Town of Lexington, Massachusetts*, Boston, Massachusetts: 1868.

Ketchum, Richard M., *Decisive Day*, New York, New York: Anchor Books, 1962.

Langguth, A.J., *Patriots: The Men Who Started the American Revolution*, New York, New York: Simon and Schuster, 1988.

Lewis, Alonzo and Newhall, James P., *History of Lynn, Essex County, Massachusetts 1629 - 1864*,

Salem, Massachusetts: Higginson Book Company, 1865.

MiddleKauff, Robert, *The Glorious Cause: The American Revolution, 1763 - 1789*, New York, New York: Oxford University Press, 1982.

Murdock, Harold, *The Nineteenth of April 1775*, Boston, Massachusetts: Mifflin Houghton Company, 1925.

Neumann, George C. and Kravic, Frank J., *Collector's Illustrated Encyclopedia of the American Revolution*, Texarkana, Texas: Schurlock Publishing Company, 1975.

Newell, John O., *Battle Road 1998*, Weston, Massachusetts: unpublished, 1998.

Phinney, Elias, *History of the Battle of Lexington on the Morning of April 1775*, Lowell, Massachusetts: Society for the Preservation of Colonial Culture, 1968.

Tourtellot, Arthur Bernon, *William Diamond's Drum: The Beginning of the War of the American Revolution*, New York, New York: W.W. Norton and Company, 1959.

Wright, Robert K., *The Continental Army*, Washington D.C.: Center of Military History, 1983.

Zobel, Hiller, *The Boston Massacre*, New York, New York: W.W. Norton and Company, 1970.

INDEX

Lightning Source UK Ltd.
Milton Keynes UK
UKHW041439190421
382249UK00001B/240

9 781312 438965